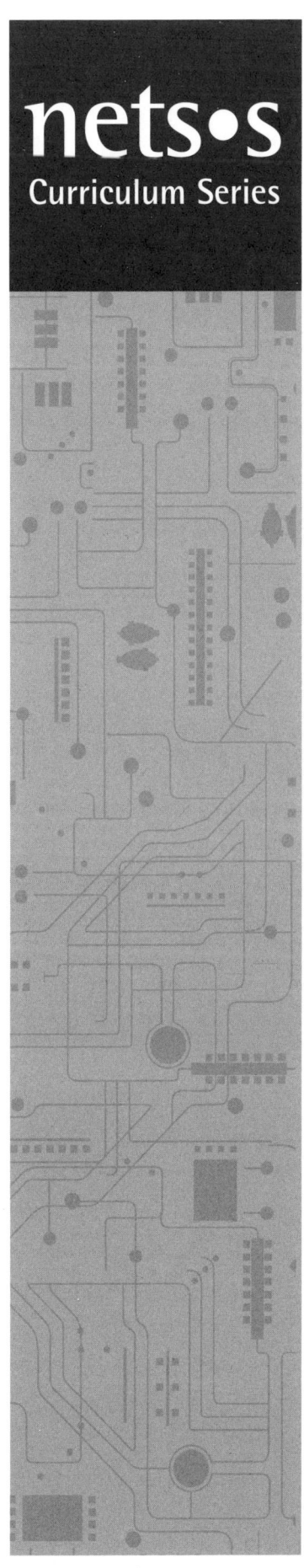

nets•s Curriculum Series

National Educational Technology Standards for Students

Social Studies Units for Grades 9–12

Walter McKenzie, Editor
Donna Archibald
Deborah Aufdenspring
Michael Hutchison
Mathew Manweller
Christopher Moersch
Patricia Terry
Cyndy Jones Woods

INTERNATIONAL SOCIETY FOR TECHNOLOGY IN EDUCATION
EUGENE, OREGON

Social Studies Units for Grades 9–12

Walter McKenzie, Editor

Donna Archibald, Deborah Aufdenspring, Michael Hutchison, Mathew Manweller, Christopher Moersch, Patricia Terry, Cyndy Jones Woods

DIRECTOR OF PUBLISHING
Jean Marie Hall

COPY EDITOR
Lynne Ertle

ACQUISITIONS EDITOR
Scott Harter

COVER DESIGN
Signe Landin

PRODUCTION EDITOR
Tracy Cozzens

BOOK DESIGN
Katherine Getta

PRODUCTION COORDINATOR
Amy Miller

LAYOUT AND PRODUCTION
Tracy Cozzens

COPYRIGHT © 2004 INTERNATIONAL SOCIETY FOR TECHNOLOGY IN EDUCATION

World rights reserved. No part of this book may be reproduced or transmitted in any form or by any means—electronic, mechanical, photocopying, recording, or otherwise—without prior written permission from the publisher. For permission, ISTE members contact Permissions Editor, ISTE, 480 Charnelton Street, Eugene, OR 97401-2626; fax: 1.541.434.8948; e-mail: permissions@iste.org. Nonmembers contact Copyright Clearance Center, 222 Rosewood Drive, Danvers, MA 01923; fax: 1.978.750.4744.

An exception to the above statement is made for K–12 classroom materials or teacher training materials contained in this publication and, if applicable, on the accompanying CD-ROM. An individual classroom teacher or teacher educator may reproduce these materials for the classroom or for student use. The reproduction of any materials appearing in this publication or on an accompanying CD-ROM for use by an entire school or school system, or for other than nonprofit educational purposes, is strictly prohibited.

Trademarks: Rather than put a trademark symbol with every occurrence of a trademarked name, we state that we are using the names only in an editorial fashion and to the benefit of the trademark owner, with no intention of infringement of the trademark.

International Society for Technology in Education (ISTE)
480 Charnelton Street
Eugene, OR 97401-2626
Order Desk: 1.800.336.5191
Order Fax: 1.541.302.3778
Customer Service: orders@iste.org
Books and Courseware: books@iste.org
Permissions: permissions@iste.org
World Wide Web: www.iste.org

First Edition
ISBN 1-56484-212-6

about iste

The International Society for Technology in Education (ISTE) is a nonprofit professional organization with a worldwide membership of leaders in educational technology. We are dedicated to promoting appropriate uses of information technology to support and improve learning, teaching, and administration in K–12 education and teacher education. As part of that mission, ISTE provides high-quality and timely information, services, and materials, such as this book.

The ISTE Publishing Department works with experienced educators to develop and produce classroom-tested books and courseware. We look for content that emphasizes the use of technology where it can make a difference—making the teacher's job easier; saving time; motivating students; helping students who have unique learning styles, abilities, or backgrounds; and creating learning environments that would be impossible without technology. We believe technology can improve the effectiveness of teaching while making learning exciting and fun.

Every manuscript and product we select for publication is peer reviewed and professionally edited. While we take pride in our publications, we also recognize the difficulties of maintaining quality while keeping on top of the latest technologies and research. Please let us know which products you would find helpful. We value your feedback on this book and other ISTE products. E-mail us at **books@iste.org**.

ISTE is home of the National Educational Technology Standards (NETS) Project, the National Educational Computing Conference (NECC), and the National Center for Preparing Tomorrow's Teachers to Use Technology (NCPT^3). To learn more about NETS or request a print catalog, visit our Web site at **www.iste.org**, which provides:

- Current educational technology standards for PK–12 students, teachers, and administrators
- A bookstore with online ordering and membership discount options
- *Learning & Leading with Technology* magazine and the *Journal of Research on Technology in Education*
- *ISTE Update,* online membership newsletter
- Teacher resources
- Discussion groups
- Professional development services, including national conference information
- Research projects
- Member services

about the authors

EDITOR

WALTER MCKENZIE has been integrating technology into instruction over the past two decades. He has a particular interest in how the Internet can promote online collaboration, cooperation, and understanding among cultures and across geographic barriers, through the use of online collaborative projects, virtual field trips, WebQuests, and other approaches to online learning. His One and Only Surfaquarium site includes innovative teaching resources, multiple intelligence pages, newsletters, online courses, and projects such as the 2004 National CyberConvention, the Presidents' Project, art and architecture, and the eIditarod. He has written, published, and presented to educators around the nation on multiple intelligences, technology integration, and creative education. He is the director of information systems for Salem Public Schools in Massachusetts. He is also the author of the book *Multiple Intelligences and Instructional Technology: A Manual for Every Mind* (ISTE, 2002).

LEAD AUTHORS

DONNA ARCHIBALD has more than 20 years of experience in education that encompasses elementary, secondary, and special education. She has held such technology positions as elementary technology consultant, curriculum/technology coordinator for special education, national Marco Polo trainer, and director of technology. Donna is currently the instructional technology coordinator for Township High School District 214 in Illinois. She has presented at many conferences including NECC, ICE, Closing the Gap, and the Illinois Technology Conference. She co-authored the book *AppleWorks: Simple Projects Primary* and was a contributing author of *Integrating Technology into the Curriculum*.

MICHAEL HUTCHISON is the technology curriculum facilitator for Vincennes Community Schools in Indiana, and is a former social studies teacher on both the high school and university levels. He has won several state, national, and international awards for his work integrating technology into the classroom, including ISTE's Outstanding Technology Using Educator and the Indiana Computer Educators Teacher of the Year for 2002. He was also named Teacher of the Year (Central U.S. Region) by *Technology and Learning Magazine* in 1999. He has written several lesson plans for PBS, as well as many activity books for Social Studies School Service. He is a faculty member for Connected University, a member of the C-SPAN Curriculum Advisory Team, and a past member of the PBS TeacherSource Advisory Group.

ABOUT THE AUTHORS

MATHEW MANWELLER is an assistant professor of political science at Central Washington University in Ellensburg, Washington. He received his doctorate from the University of Oregon in 2003. Before entering academia, he spent seven years as a high school social studies teacher in the Pacific Northwest, where he helped found Silver Creek Alternative School, the first Idaho charter school for at-risk students. He received his teaching credentials from Whitman College in 1991. He has written several scholarly articles on constitutional law, tort reform, and direct democracy as well as the economics textbook *Thinking Economics.*

CYNDY JONES WOODS has taught homeless, transient, and at-risk students for the past 12 years. She serves as an adjunct faculty member at a community college and for Connected University, where she also manages 35 adjunct faculty as faculty manager. She is a Fulbright Teacher Scholar and Fulbright Master Teacher who spent time in Japan working with instructors, teaching at Hiroshima Mitsuzugaoka High School, and developing peace education in Hiroshima. She also worked in the Galapagos Islands as part of a research project through the University of Arizona, studying indigenous marine iguanas.

CHAPTER AUTHORS

DEBORAH AUFDENSPRING is a classroom teacher and consultant who conducts workshops in project-based learning and in integrating technology into curricula. She also has made many presentations around the country about her innovative humanities curriculum. She was one of the teachers who opened New Technology High School in Napa, California, and after teaching there for its first four years, moved to Minnesota to help open the Minnesota Business Academy in Saint Paul. The next school she is helping to establish is the Mare Island Technology Academy High School in Vallejo, California.

CHRISTOPHER MOERSCH is co-founder and director of the National Business Education Alliance in Corvallis, Oregon—a nonprofit organization devoted to improving student academic achievement as well as the level of technology use in the classroom. He is a past school administrator and classroom teacher from southern California. As a researcher and national consultant, he has lectured and written extensively on technology implementation, curriculum design, and performance assessment. He is the author of the book *Beyond Hardware: Using Existing Technology to Promote Higher-Level Thinking* (ISTE, 2002).

PATRICIA TERRY is a former classroom teacher and district technology coordinator with 31 years of experience in public education. She is an educational technology consultant specializing in the integration of technology into classroom instruction. She also serves as an adjunct instructor in instructional technology for Virginia Wesleyan College, and facilitates online courses targeting instructional technology strategies for Classroom Connect's Connected University and PBS's TeacherLine.

contents

Introduction 1
The NETS Project 1
Essential Conditions for Technology Integration 3
How to Use This Book 5
Beyond This Book 6
Reference 6

Section 1—Strategies for Getting Started 7

CHAPTER 1 ■ Levels of Technology Integration 9
Christopher Moersch

CHAPTER 2 ■ Project- and Problem-Based Learning 11
Deborah Aufdenspring

CHAPTER 3 ■ Successful Searching in Social Studies 17
Patricia Terry

CHAPTER 4 ■ Constructing a Rubric 25
Walter McKenzie

Section 2—Resource Units 31

The Seven Pillars of the Constitution 33
Mathew Manweller

A Flash Tapestry: A Digital Study of the Battle of Hastings 43
Walter McKenzie

The Civil War: A Multimedia Investigation 51
Michael Hutchison

Money, Special Interest Groups, and Reelection Rates 65
Mathew Manweller

Gross Domestic Product and World Events 75
Donna Archibald

How Social Are We Anyway? 87
Cyndy Jones Woods

Virtual Reality, Cultural Reality: A Study of the Middle East 101
Walter McKenzie

Political Polling: Measuring Support for Environmental Policies 109
Mathew Manweller

The Modern Presidency 121
Michael Hutchison

All the World in an Archipelago 135
Cyndy Jones Woods

Many Shades Are We: An Examination of the Diverse Cultures
That Make Up America 155
Donna Archibald

From *Plessy* to *Brown*: Concept Mapping the U.S. Supreme Court 165
Mathew Manweller

Prisoner's Dilemma: A Wireless Simulation of the Romanov Court 175
Walter McKenzie

Appendix **185**

National Educational Technology Standards for Students (NETS•S) 186
National Educational Technology Standards for Teachers (NETS•T) 187
National Educational Technology Standards for Administrators (NETS•A) 189
Social Studies Standards 191

introduction

The NETS Project

The National Educational Technology Standards (NETS) Project was initiated by the Accreditation and Professional Standards Committee of the International Society for Technology in Education (ISTE). ISTE has emerged as a recognized leader among professional organizations for educators involved with technology. ISTE's mission is to promote appropriate uses of technology to support and improve learning, teaching, and administration. Its members are leaders in educational technology, including teachers, technology coordinators, education administrators, and teacher educators. ISTE supports all subject area disciplines by providing publications, conferences, online resources, and services that help educators combine the knowledge and skills of their teaching fields with the application of technologies to improve learning and teaching.

The primary goal of the NETS Project is to enable stakeholders in PK–12 education to develop national standards for the educational uses of technology that facilitate school improvement in the United States. The NETS Project is developing standards to guide educational leaders in recognizing and addressing the essential conditions for the effective use of technology to support PK–12 education.

The NETS for Students (NETS•S) Curriculum Series Project represents a continuation of ISTE's desire to provide educators with the means to implement the NETS. *Social Studies Units for Grades 9–12* is specifically designed to provide high school teachers with curriculum to meet the Grades 9–12 performance indicators of the NETS.

NATIONAL EDUCATIONAL TECHNOLOGY STANDARDS FOR STUDENTS

The NETS for Students are divided into six broad categories. Standards within each category are to be introduced, reinforced, and mastered by students. These categories provide a framework for linking performance indicators, listed by grade level, to the standards. Teachers can use these standards and profiles as guidelines for planning technology-based activities in which students achieve success in learning, communication, and life skills.

1. **Basic operations and concepts**
    - Students demonstrate a sound understanding of the nature and operation of technology systems.
    - Students are proficient in the use of technology.

2. **Social, ethical, and human issues**
    - Students understand the ethical, cultural, and societal issues related to technology.

INTRODUCTION

- Students practice responsible use of technology systems, information, and software.
- Students develop positive attitudes toward technology uses that support lifelong learning, collaboration, personal pursuits, and productivity.

3. **Technology productivity tools**
   - Students use technology tools to enhance learning, increase productivity, and promote creativity.
   - Students use productivity tools to collaborate in constructing technology-enhanced models, preparing publications, and producing other creative works.

4. **Technology communications tools**
   - Students use telecommunications to collaborate, publish, and interact with peers, experts, and other audiences.
   - Students use a variety of media and formats to communicate information and ideas effectively to multiple audiences.

5. **Technology research tools**
   - Students use technology to locate, evaluate, and collect information from a variety of sources.
   - Students use technology tools to process data and report results.
   - Students evaluate and select new information resources and technological innovations based on the appropriateness to specific tasks.

6. **Technology problem-solving and decision-making tools**
   - Students use technology resources for solving problems and making informed decisions.
   - Students employ technology in the development of strategies for solving problems in the real world.

PERFORMANCE INDICATORS, GRADES 9–12

All students should have opportunities to demonstrate the following performances. Numbers in parentheses following each performance indicator refer to the standards category to which the performance is linked. ISTE has developed performance indicators for all grade levels. However, the following material presents only the Grades 9–12 indicators, the specific focus of this book.

Prior to completion of Grade 12, students will:

1. Identify capabilities and limitations of contemporary and emerging technology resources and assess the potential of these systems and services to address personal, lifelong learning, and workplace needs. (2)

2. Make informed choices among technology systems, resources, and services. (1, 2)

3. Analyze advantages and disadvantages of widespread use of and reliance on technology in the workplace and in society as a whole. (2)

4. Demonstrate and advocate for legal and ethical behavior among peers, family, and community regarding the use of technology and information. (2)

5. Use technology tools and resources for managing and communicating personal/professional information (e.g., finances, schedules, addresses, purchases, correspondence). (3, 4)

6. Evaluate technology-based options, including distance and distributed education, for lifelong learning. (5)

7. Routinely and efficiently use online information resources to meet needs for collaboration, research, publications, communications, and productivity. (4, 5, 6)

8. Select and apply technology tools for research, information analysis, problem solving, and decision making in content learning. (4, 5)

9. Investigate and apply expert systems, intelligent agents, and simulations in real-world situations. (3, 5, 6)

10. Collaborate with peers, experts, and others to contribute a content-related knowledge base by using technology to compile, synthesize, produce, and disseminate information, models, and other creative works. (4, 5, 6)

Section 2 provides 13 social studies resource units. This technology-embedded curriculum is specifically designed to help students meet these performance indicators.

Essential Conditions for Technology Integration

Successful learning activities, such as the ones provided in this book, depend on more than just the technology. Certain conditions are necessary for schools to effectively use technology for learning, teaching, and educational management. Physical, pedagogical, financial, and policy dimensions greatly affect the success of technology use in schools.

The curriculum provided in this book will be more effective if a combination of essential conditions for creating learning environments conducive to powerful uses of technology is achieved, including:

- vision with support and proactive leadership from the education system;
- educators skilled in the use of technology for learning;
- content standards and curriculum resources;
- student-centered approaches to learning;
- assessment of the effectiveness of technology for learning;
- access to contemporary technologies, software, and telecommunications networks;
- technical assistance for maintaining and using technology resources;
- community partners who provide expertise, support, and real-life interactions;

INTRODUCTION

- ongoing financial support for sustained technology use; and
- policies and standards supporting new learning environments.

Traditional educational practices no longer provide students with all the necessary skills for economic survival in today's workplace. Students today must apply strategies for solving problems using appropriate tools for learning, collaborating, and communicating. The following chart lists characteristics representing traditional approaches to learning and corresponding strategies associated with new learning environments.

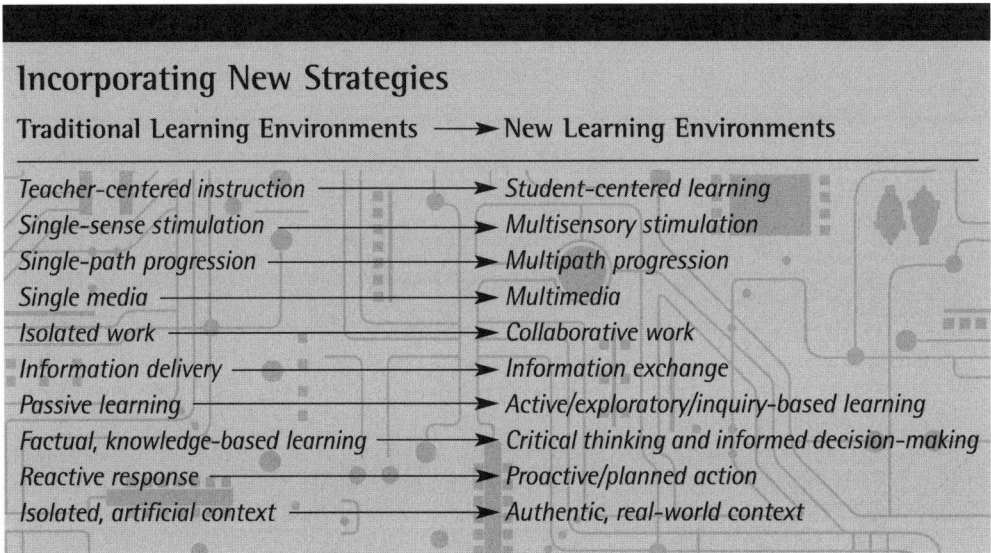

Incorporating New Strategies

Traditional Learning Environments	→	New Learning Environments
Teacher-centered instruction	→	Student-centered learning
Single-sense stimulation	→	Multisensory stimulation
Single-path progression	→	Multipath progression
Single media	→	Multimedia
Isolated work	→	Collaborative work
Information delivery	→	Information exchange
Passive learning	→	Active/exploratory/inquiry-based learning
Factual, knowledge-based learning	→	Critical thinking and informed decision-making
Reactive response	→	Proactive/planned action
Isolated, artificial context	→	Authentic, real-world context

The most effective learning environments meld traditional approaches and new approaches to facilitate learning of relevant content while addressing individual needs. The resulting learning environments should prepare students to:

- communicate using a variety of media and formats;
- access and exchange information in a variety of ways;
- compile, organize, analyze, and synthesize information;
- draw conclusions and make generalizations based on information gathered;
- know content and be able to locate additional information as needed;
- become self-directed learners;
- collaborate and cooperate in team efforts; and
- interact with others in ethical and appropriate ways.

Teachers know that the wise use of technology can enrich learning environments and enable students to achieve marketable skills. We hope that high school educators will find the curriculum and other material provided within helpful in meeting these goals.

How to Use This Book

Social Studies Units for Grades 9–12 is divided into two main sections.

SECTION 1—STRATEGIES FOR GETTING STARTED

Section 1 provides chapters that will help teachers successfully integrate technology into high school classrooms. Teachers are provided with background on levels of technology integration. Teachers also are given ideas on developing project- and problem-based learning activities, incorporating the responsible and effective use of the Internet into the classroom, and creating rubrics.

SECTION 2—RESOURCE UNITS

Section 2 provides teachers with 13 resource units based on diverse and engaging concepts in social studies. For each unit, a day-by-day teaching plan is provided, along with the NETS•S and social studies standards addressed, the unit objectives, the central discipline area, a unit description, and assessment strategies. In addition, each unit offers the following six Unit Tools:

INTERDISCIPLINARY LINKS	The units are designed to be interdisciplinary. Each unit identifies a variety of ways teachers can bring other content areas into the lesson.
SPOTLIGHT ON TECHNOLOGY	Each unit highlights the use of one or more types of technology. The Spotlight on Technology section explains how the highlighted technology can be incorporated into the lesson plan.
TECHNOLOGY RESOURCES NEEDED	Each unit provides a list of all the hardware and software needed to successfully implement the lesson.
WEB, LITERATURE, AND VIDEO RESOURCES	Many of the units expect that students have access to the Internet. This tool gives the teacher a list of important Web sites that can be used to enhance the lesson. All the units focus on a multidisciplinary approach to teaching. Because reading and writing are so important, each unit also offers a list of books teachers may want to use in conjunction with the lesson. In addition, some of the lessons suggest video resources that can be used to augment student understanding of the topic.
TEACHING TIPS	It always helps to have suggestions on the best way to implement a lesson. This tool suggests ways a teacher can get the most out of the lesson. This section provides insights into which teaching strategy might be most effective for you.
LESSON EXTENDERS	Sometimes lessons are so good, students and teachers don't want them to end. Each unit offers suggestions for extending the lesson for those of you interested in further exploring the topic.
ASSESSMENT	At the end of each unit is a complete assessment rubric keyed to the NETS for Students and the social studies standards from the National Council for the Social Studies.

INTRODUCTION

APPENDIX

The appendix provides the NETS for students, teachers, and administrators, as well as the social studies standards.

Beyond This Book

Keep in mind that the authors of individual learning activities could not address the needs of every teaching situation. Take the examples presented and modify them to fit your circumstances and needs. The sample lessons also provide a lens for re-examining traditional lessons and discovering ways to infuse technology to enrich teaching and learning. As you are inspired to create new lessons and units, please share these with others by posting them on the ISTE Web site (**www.iste.org**). But that's not all!

Be proactive about sharing your good work with others. There are many lesson plan Web sites as well as school, district, professional association, and parent meetings at which to present new lesson plans and the resulting student work. Educators need to learn from their peers. Educators also need to inform parents of their efforts to integrate technology and learning, and to inform the greater public about how schools are meeting the needs of students, parents, and the community.

Reference

ISTE. (1998). *National educational technology standards for students.* Eugene, OR: Author. Also available online at **http://cnets.iste.org/students/s_stands.html**.

section 1

Strategies for Getting Started

CHAPTER 1 ■ Levels of Technology Integration
Christopher Moersch

CHAPTER 2 ■ Project- and Problem-Based Learning
Deborah Aufdenspring

CHAPTER 3 ■ Successful Searching in Social Studies
Patricia Terry

CHAPTER 4 ■ Constructing a Rubric
Walter McKenzie

CHRISTOPHER MOERSCH

Levels of Technology Integration

Eight years ago I created a conceptual framework called LoTI (Levels of Technology Implementation) to classify the ways teachers use technology in the classroom. The eight categories of technology implementation range from Level 0 (Nonuse) to Level 6 (Refinement). The genesis for this system dates back to the works of David Dwyer with ACOT as well as Gene Hall and Susan Louck's efforts with CBAM (Concerns-Based Adoption Model). What I learned from these early pioneers in instructional technology and change theory, respectively, was that adaptations in technology use are significantly dependent on teachers' personal concerns governing their acceptance of a new innovation.

To a large measure these personal concerns are rooted in a teacher's belief system surrounding instruction, student assessment, and learning theory. If this is the case, then how can we change such attitudes and thus improve technology use practices in the classroom? However, a more immediate and pragmatic question is "*Why* attempt to change these attitudes?"

In response to the latter question, recent studies have pinpointed the positive effect of higher cognitive processing skills, relevant learning experiences, and student-centered curricula on student academic achievement. Yet the traditional subject matter-based approach characterized by lectures, teacher-led presentations, sequential and uniform learning activities, and traditional measures of student evaluation still dominate the educational landscape.

Not surprisingly, the same classroom processes are mirrored in current uses of technology. Based on a sampling of 250,000 teachers who completed the LoTI Technology Use Assessment, approximately 67% self-assessed themselves at Levels 0–2. Level 0 (Nonuse), Level 1 (Awareness), and Level 2 (Exploration) are characterized by the use of multimedia presentations to augment lectures, the assignment of multimedia projects that support lower levels of student cognition (such as knowledge and comprehension), and the superficial application of technology to meet some disjointed and vague local technology implementation standard.

Changing Attitudes

Regarding the question about how we can change attitudes about teaching and learning, my response is that we must (1) become instructional technology connoisseurs and (2) provide teachers with exemplary resources that align with these higher levels of technology implementation. As instructional technology connoisseurs, all stakeholders including teachers, instructional specialists, and administrators are able to distinguish higher levels of technology use from their lower level counterparts and, more important, recognize when the higher levels of technology use are necessary based on the learner's readiness, interests, and learning profile. These higher levels—represented by LoTI Level 3 (Infusion), Levels 4A and 4B (Integration), Level 5 (Expansion), and Level 6 (Refinement)—are characterized by Web-based projects that focus on higher order thinking skills (application, analysis, synthesis, evaluation), student-centered curricula involving real-world problems and solutions, and the use of productivity tools (such as spreadsheets, databases, and graphic organizers) that enable students to make inferences and draw conclusions. These uses of technology are the ones linked to improved student achievement on standardized tests.

Equipping Teachers

Equipping teachers with the resources to model technology use at the higher LoTI levels is the pivotal challenge confronting us. The units of instruction offered in *Social Studies Units for Grades 9–12* articulate specific approaches for integrating higher order thinking skills with technology use in the social studies classroom. As you read through the various instructional units, ranging from money in U.S. elections to the gross domestic product, you will note that each unit focuses on appropriate uses of technology that inspire students to demonstrate both higher order thinking skills and complex thinking strategies. Teachers are encouraged to use a myriad of technology tools, including spreadsheets, concept-mapping software, Internet resources, presentation programs, and digital video cameras. You will also note that each unit provides step-by-step guidelines and options for implementing each unit.

As educators, we are continually mining the Internet in search of content-rich lessons that motivate students to learn and take advantage of the existing technology infrastructure. Yet most teachers will readily admit that the lack of time is their greatest barrier to using technology effectively in the classroom. Our collective charge then is locating exemplary resources and teaching strategies that will enable teachers to begin the process of changing their current belief systems and in doing so realize the benefits that technology has to offer. *Social Studies Units for Grades 9–12* accomplishes that mission.

chapter 2

DEBORAH AUFDENSPRING

Project- and Problem-Based Learning

Watching project- and problem-based learning take place in a classroom underscores their significant differences from usual classroom practices. One might see small groups of students talking quietly, laughing, or practicing a presentation. Others might be hunched over computer screens discussing the data displayed on the monitor, or students might move among groups discussing common issues. It may even be difficult to find the teacher as she melds into a group of students, making suggestions but not directing their activities. Rarely in such a classroom are students playing at their desks, passing notes, falling asleep, or asking for passes out of the room. Rather, most of the students are relaxed and yet maintain an attentive seriousness—an attitude that this is real work, deserving of respectful attention. Such behavior is the result of teachers who keep reading and lecturing to a minimum in favor of more compelling activities. Some teachers even forgo traditional testing modes, relying solely on students' projects for assessment.

The philosophical underpinnings of project- and problem-based learning are built on the constructivist theories and research of Piaget, Dewey, Bruner, and Taba. Project-based learning clearly creates the conditions for students to take charge of their own learning and generate their own knowledge from a great variety of information sources.

Project- and problem-based learning can be considered two ends of a spectrum of constructivist learning. In project-based learning, conditions may be more clearly delineated than in problem-based learning, but they still leave students with wide latitude for determining the course of their learning. Problem-based learning is messier and asks students to reformulate their hypotheses in the midst of solving a problem.

What Is Project-Based Learning?

Project-based learning is a model for teaching that focuses on the major concepts of a curriculum, involving students in meaningful investigations of those concepts. Concepts may be introduced by a teacher and supported by texts, speakers, and other sources. Students then work autonomously to create projects that demonstrate their learning to teachers, peers, and the community.

CONTENT
: Compelling and complex ideas and projects are presented to students, who are then required to cope with their ambiguity. These are real-world problems that students care about; the problems presented often cross content area lines.

ACTIVITIES
: As they encounter and analyze these projects, students investigate many facets of issues while they search for valid research resources. As students make connections among ideas, they develop new skills and work on a variety of tasks, often in cooperative work groups. Students use the tools of the real world to complete their investigations, and often those tools include the wide variety of classroom technologies available: software applications, projection devices, the Internet, e-mail, and multimedia. As students investigate, they get feedback from coaches and experts about the validity of their ideas and sources.

CONDITIONS
: Project-based learning underscores students' autonomy as they take part in inquiry and pursue solutions in a cooperative social context. Projects are lengthy and require students to develop and use time management skills, both individually and as part of a group. In taking on the tasks of researchers, reporters, planners, managers, and other roles, students direct their own work and take control of their own learning.

RESULTS
: Project-based learning results in real-world outcomes as students create models, reports, multimedia presentations, skits, and other products that demonstrate what they have learned. Students are responsible for determining how they are going to demonstrate knowledge with peers, and the students themselves take part in assessing their projects. A project analysis sheet and class discussion can facilitate such assessment. As students engage in these activities, they often show growth in social skills and self-management, and a disposition for learning on their own—the skills promoted by the 1991 Secretary's Commission on Achieving Necessary Skills (SCANS) report. The full SCANS report can be found at http://wdr.doleta.gov/SCANS/whatwork/whatwork.html.

AN EXAMPLE OF PROJECT-BASED LEARNING

To introduce the following project to students, the teacher would assign the group to be members of President Washington's cabinet after the Revolutionary War. Students would then be asked to advise the new president on how to bring the country together in setting up a new government. With a history of strong ties to the British, the new nation has citizens whose relatives still reside on the British Isles.

CONTENT
: Students research the causes and consequences of the Revolutionary War as well as information about the people who lived during that time. This would cross the curricular areas of social studies, economics, literature, and ethics and could require delving into art and music.

ACTIVITIES
: Students gather and analyze information regarding the issues from textbooks, library reference material, and historical sites on the Internet. Taking that information into account, students hypothesize about various scenarios and then come up with advice for Washington.

CONDITIONS Students engage in independent and group investigations of this post-Revolutionary War scenario. They determine for themselves how they will fulfill the project requirements, noting that there is no "right" answer—only rigorous thinking—required in their end product. Students select and analyze their own resources, determining which are most valid. Work is collaborative with teams of students and with outside resources.

RESULTS Students determine their own end product to demonstrate their learning. Such projects might be as varied as a debate, a multimedia report on the consequences of cutting off all ties with the British, a written report on the discussion of personal rights, or a presentation on how the country might be if the British had won. Regardless of the end product, students will have shown that they can evaluate sources for historical accuracy or bias, that they can make decisions about which sources to use, and that they understand ambiguity in real-world problems.

ADVANTAGES OF PROJECT-BASED LEARNING

The overall advantages of project-based learning are that students become responsible for their own learning and that their learning is presented in an authentic manner. Learning becomes relevant and personal to students as they become increasingly competent at searching for answers and solving real-world problems. Additionally, project-based learning allows information to be connected to students' prior knowledge as well as connected across curricula. It also promotes higher levels of cognitive processing.

Additionally, project-based learning supports meeting the individual student learning needs. Project-based learning accommodates different intelligences among students and allows them to demonstrate their knowledge in ways that take advantage of those intelligences. The end products may highlight musical, artistic, technology, language, acting, or other skills. Collaborative and social skills are also promoted as students work in groups in noncompetitive settings.

Students become the owners of new knowledge as they defend their positions to their peers and others. Gaining knowledge by making connections with prior experience in a social setting remains with students.

Finally, project-based learning and technology experience can build on each other as technology skills are used to solve real-world problems. For many students, this use of technology is intrinsically motivating and a good match with project-based learning. When students need to solve real-world problems, they need to do so with real-world tools. The Internet provides students access to resources, both print and human, as well as primary source documents. Students engaged in project-based learning activities have received responses from scientists, artists, and participants in historical events. Additionally, computing power allows students to cope with the huge amounts of data that must be analyzed across many projects. And finally, sophisticated presentation tools encourage students to create professional presentations to demonstrate their understanding.

DISADVANTAGES OF PROJECT-BASED LEARNING

Launching project-based learning for the first time can be a difficult transition for both students and teachers who are accustomed to a traditional approach. The change from essays, reports, multiple choice tests, and the like is akin to going through a cultural shift. It is difficult, especially for students who have learned how to get good grades on tests and papers. Creating projects requires quite different skill sets than the traditional means of assessment; it is not unlikely that such students will plead for a return to quizzes, tests, and the things "real teachers" do as they fear the unfamiliar territory of being responsible for creating the solution rather than being told there is only one way to be correct.

For teachers, it may be difficult to step aside and give students more control over their own learning, particularly because this does not mean less teacher preparation. Guiding students through tasks, constructing cooperative learning groups, and grading complicated projects are both time-consuming and complex. There is no crystal clear "right answer" as found in a multiple-choice test.

Perhaps the most common criticism of project-based learning is that it sacrifices breadth for depth in covering materials. This is particularly problematic for districts that overly emphasize standardized test scores. Some of this concern can be ameliorated by carefully constructing projects that meet state and national standards. Nonetheless, higher test scores do not always follow, and the criticism stands.

It is also more difficult and time-consuming to obtain evidence of a student's knowledge and understanding, particularly because grading must be done on many levels: language skills, technology skills, presentation skills, research skills, and group skills. Not only is assessment time-consuming, the time required for teachers to suggest or create projects can take many more hours than a lecture and multiple-choice test. Some of this time, but not all, can be recouped as students work independently on projects with teachers advising but not directing them. However, the preparation reflects the complexity of the projects themselves.

What Is Problem-Based Learning?

Problem-based learning is a curricular approach that develops problem-solving ability, interdisciplinary knowledge, and cross-curricular skills. Its first application was in medical schools, where students solved real-world problems in diagnosis and treatment. In problem-based learning, students are confronted with a messy, ill-defined problem with insufficient information and the necessity to determine the best solution possible in a limited time. This structure develops problem-solving abilities, a specific knowledge base, and inquiry skills. It is student-centered, as teachers give only guidelines for how to solve problems. Problem-based learning assignments, like those for project-based learning, are evaluated on performance. Likewise, the content, activities, conditions, and results are similar to those of project-based learning.

AN EXAMPLE OF PROBLEM-BASED LEARNING

Problem-based learning is usually introduced with an "entry document" that defines the students' roles in a real-life problem. The entry document, which loosely defines the problem and the students' task, is written as a real-world document might be. In this case, a group of students will be given the role of consultants to the U.S. Fish and Wildlife Service and asked to create a plan to reintroduce wolves to Yellowstone National Park.

CONTENT — Students research Yellowstone National Park, ranching on the park's boundaries, the views of those who live and work near the park, the environmental requirements for wolf packs, and the reasons the wolves are no longer in the area.

ACTIVITIES — Students may conduct research by accessing national park sites on the World Wide Web, by interviewing local national park rangers, by interviewing national park employees through e-mail, by talking to local ranchers or farmers about predation, as well as by conducting research in the numerous standard ways using libraries and texts. When students have done their research and come up with a plan, a new element is introduced to the problem.

This introduction of new information is a major facet that distinguishes problem-based learning from project-based learning. Students may, for example, be told that hearings on their wolf reintroduction plan resulted in overwhelming negative testimony. Students are apprised of the testimony (which may be engendered by other groups of students) and are then required to assess the criticisms as they come in, alter their hypotheses, and come up with a new solution to the plan to reintroduce wolves.

CONDITIONS — Students in this scenario need to analyze data for accuracy and make determinations about the validity and usefulness of the data. They need to cope with ambiguity as they reorganize and synthesize information. Students are given wide latitude on how to search for information, and the role of the teacher remains that of a guide—one of many experts or sources that may be accessed for information. As students work, they handle multiple perspectives on the reintroduction scenario and learn to read and listen carefully, assessing multiple pieces of information.

PERFORMANCE — As in project-based learning, the end product of problem-based learning is a performance that synthesizes information and presents it to peers and the community. In this case, the product is the revised plan for reintroducing wolves to Yellowstone. The product is graded on the extent to which students took the complexity of the situation into account. It would also be graded for language skills, presentation techniques, group work, technology aptitude, and research abilities.

ADVANTAGES OF PROBLEM-BASED LEARNING

Students who engage in problem-based learning acquire several life skills. They must develop a variety of hypotheses as they find, evaluate, and use data from multiple sources. They learn to integrate numerous perspectives and discover that in the real world, "right answers" are rare to nonexistent. Students must alter hypotheses as new information becomes available and must find solutions based on clear reasoning, using information that fits the problem. Additionally, they learn cooperative skills as they work in groups to solve these problems. They develop an appreciation for other points of view, and they develop the ability to defend their own points of view. As in project-based learning, the learning becomes their own.

DISADVANTAGES OF PROBLEM-BASED LEARNING

Problem-based learning carries with it the same disadvantages of project-based learning. Breadth is necessarily sacrificed for depth, it requires complex planning, and it is a cultural shift for both students and teachers. Additionally, it is more difficult to obtain evidence of students' knowledge.

Conclusion

Both project- and problem-based learning are based on students' active inquiry. By evaluating new ideas, relating cross-curricular concepts, and working cooperatively, students engage in higher order thinking skills. Projects and problems usually are intrinsically interesting to students, leading them to use a variety of real-world tools and resources creatively to produce imaginative end products. Students become empowered to take charge of their own learning, and when that happens, much of the resistance to schooling evaporates. It is not uncommon for teachers to report students who come early to school, want to miss recess, stay late, and even ask that school be opened on weekends so that they can work on projects. Students become self-directed learners and carry the skills and attitudes they learn from project- and problem-based learning into other areas of their lives.

References

Aufdenspring, Deborah. (2000, July). *Project-based learning: A deliberate design for learning*. Workshop conducted for Montgomery Schools, Brewster Technology High School, Montgomery, Alabama.

Buck Institute. (n.d.). *Overview: Project-based learning*. Retrieved from **www.bie.org/pbl/index.php**

Illinois Mathematics and Science Academy, Center for Problem-Based Learning. (2001, April 10). *What is problem-based learning?* Retrieved from **www.imsa.edu/team/cpbl/problem.html**

Maxwell, Nan L., Bellisimo, Yolanda, & Mergendoller, John. (1999). *Problem-based learning: Modifying the medical school model for teaching high school economics*. Proceedings of the American Educational Research Association, Session 3:08.

Schools of California Online Resources for Education. (n.d.). *Problem-based learning*. Retrieved from **http://score.rims.k12.ca.us/problearn.html**

Secretary's Commission on Achieving Necessary Skills. (1991). *What work requires of schools: A SCANS report for America 2000*. Washington, D.C.: Author. Also available online at **http://wdr.doleta.gov/SCANS/whatwork/whatwork.html**

PATRICIA TERRY

Successful Searching in Social Studies

Social studies offerings at the secondary level span diverse topics ranging from the historical events of the past to the current events of today. Students are exposed to issues delivered through a wide variety of media including textbooks, periodicals, newspapers, television, radio, movies, and Internet sites. In recent years the Internet has become a major resource for students as they conduct instructional research. Search tools are designed to categorize specific data from Web sites and databases housed on the Internet, and to make this information accessible. Even with the vast amount of data available, it can be difficult to locate information targeted to specific issues and topics, unless students are provided with guidance in how to use search tools successfully.

Search Tools

Search tools are utilities available on the Internet to help individuals locate information about specific topics. There are many different search tools available for student use. Some target specific types of documents or files. Others are designed for specific users, such as young children or business professionals. When students begin exploring the many tools available, they tend to use the same search tool for all their information needs. This may be due to their lack of exposure to other tools, and often results in identifying materials that do not adequately address the topic of the research. Search tools vary in their approach to recording Web sites in their databases, and update this information on varying schedules. Although many tools add new sites on a regular basis, few remove sites that are no longer available. As a result, using only one search tool can have a great effect on the results a student might obtain. Therefore, it is important to submit a search to several search sites to achieve the best results.

SEARCH ENGINES

Search engines are very popular and easy to use. They locate Internet resources by examining identified keywords in a document or the contents of each page, and organizing the words found. These sites are analyzed using technology to determine the placement of a specific resource within the engine's database. Each search engine establishes specific criteria for determining a target site's priority in the search engine's results. This may be based on frequency of words used, number of times a site is visited, or some other determining factor. Consequently, many searches by students result in thousands of potential resources. Popular search engines include Google, AltaVista, All the Web, and Teoma. *Metasearch engines* search several individual search engines and return the results in a compact format. Examples of metasearch engines include DogPile and iTools, which are well designed, easy to use, and return appropriate results quickly and efficiently.

Most search engines provide a basic search feature as well as an advanced search option. Although most research can be accomplished using the basic search strategy, students should be encouraged to review the process of conducting an advanced search when visiting a search engine. The directions provided allow students to become power searchers within minutes. Although the strategies employed for advanced searching are similar for each engine, they may not necessarily be exactly the same, so reviewing the procedures is necessary.

General searching can also be accessed through reference Web sites, which are designed to allow users to select from among the many resources and databases available on the Internet. Refdesk is one of the most popular sites in this category. It provides numerous links to tools targeted for specific information such as almanacs, dictionaries, encyclopedias, and other familiar reference materials. InfoPlease is similar to Refdesk and provides access to multiple search tools. An especially interesting tool found here is "This Day in History," in which students can learn about historical events occurring on a specific date. Another resource, the Internet Public Library, provides a search tool designed to assist students in locating specific resources in a one-stop location. This is a handy reference site for use in schools.

A recent development is the advent of "clustering" search engines, which categorize the results of a submitted search strategy. The user can quickly select from the appropriate categories, reducing the amount of time taken to verify unrelated links. Growing in popularity among professional educators and students is the search engine Vivisimo, which uses this clustering approach. This metasearch engine categorizes its findings and returns specialized results, including such items as a list of specific speeches made by historical figures, which is very applicable to secondary social studies.

SUBJECT DIRECTORIES

Subject directories organize Internet resources into general categories and subcategories. The assignment of a Web resource to a specific category within a directory's listing may be done through technology based on keywords in the title or description of the page, or by a person who scans the content and recommends a specific placement for that resource. Subject directories afford students the opportunity to scan through several levels within a topic to locate information. This is extremely helpful when students are not exactly sure what they want to find, and it exposes them to many possibilities for consideration in their research. It is an excellent tool to use for broad topic searches. Traditional subject directories include Yahoo! and the Educator's Reference Desk.

SUBJECT GUIDES

Subject guides organize resources on the Internet by academic subject area and are likely to be juried by professionals who have analyzed page content for inclusion in the guide. These are wonderful resources for use in classroom activities and projects. Subject guides are available at Infomine, Librarian's Index to the Internet, and Academic Info.

SPECIALIZED DATABASES

Specialized databases are repositories of specific types of information. They may contain compilations of news articles, research reports, images, video segments, speeches, and primary source documents. Specialized databases are a significant resource for social studies. The ERIC Database is an example of a specialized database.

Of special interest to social studies teachers and students are databases of primary source documents. The collection of primary sources available on the Internet is constantly growing as individuals and organizations devote the time and resources necessary for converting documents to digital formats and making them electronically accessible. Several Web resources can serve as starting points for accessing primary source documents, but it is also possible to locate primary source information by using traditional search tools.

Primary Sources on the Web provides a list of primary source Web sites and is an excellent starting point for finding primary sources to use in the classroom or as part of a research project. This list is updated regularly and includes annotations to provide the researcher with information regarding the types of documents that may be accessed at each collection site. The National Archives and Records Administration (NARA) also provides an extensive listing of primary source collections. Included at this site are sample lesson plans and activities that incorporate the use of primary source documents correlating to the National History Standards. These activities encourage students to work with images of the actual documents related to specific historical events.

Hundreds of resources for social studies may be accessed and searched at the Federal Resources for Educational Excellence Web site. The site offers an internal search tool. For example, you might search for "depression." Because your starting location was in social studies, the results are appropriately aligned with economic depression.

The Historical Text Archive houses historical documents for reference and comparison. These documents have been transferred to digital formats, making it possible to access them through the Internet. Once connected to this site, you can look for a particular document using the search window.

The Invisible Web

Many of the resources and tools described relate directly to Web sites and databases classified as being part of the "visible Web." An entire collection of additional information exists on the "invisible Web," which is generally not cataloged by traditional search tools. By encouraging students to use the Invisible Web directory, they will have access to documents, databases, and other information to enhance their understanding of a topic. The process for conducting a search of the invisible Web is identical to that for a search of the visible Web. Public records and reports of current news and events are particularly pertinent information sources located on the invisible Web.

Direct Search is another tool available to help individuals access information on the invisible Web. One subdirectory of this site, Campaign, links to speeches, news, congressional research, and campaign finance information. It is organized by individual states, with links to very current information on these topics.

Search Strategy Development

A critical skill for students, particularly at the secondary level, is the ability to define a search strategy. Teachers must provide opportunities for students to learn and strengthen their ability to construct efficient search strategies, because they will not inherently discover this skill on their own. Library and media specialists have always recognized the need to know how to locate information and are generally willing to help teachers and students learn ways to access information on the Internet efficiently. Tap their knowledge and skill by having them plan instructional activities, supply resources, and provide support for students.

As students begin to learn how to construct a search strategy, they will need to understand several key concepts.

- Keywords are more specific than subjects.
- Boolean logic can refine a search.
- Synonyms are critical. Consider other options for word choice.
- Search tools are updated regularly.

KEYWORDS

A student searching for information about the Great Depression might begin by going to Google and simply entering the word "depression." The use of the generic term depression written with a lowercase "d" would generate references to mental illness, as well as references to a technique used in the visual arts. Students could refine the search strategy for a more focused result by using the phrase "economic depression." In this case "economic depression" presents specific keywords for the search tool to use. This would limit the results to the desired information.

BOOLEAN LOGIC

By using Boolean operators (AND, NOT, OR), search results are further restricted, resulting in a list of resources that tends to be more focused on the topic. Although the words can be used within the search strategy, symbols present a shortcut to obtaining similar results. AND is represented by the plus sign (+), NOT is indicated by the minus sign (-), and OR is achieved by pressing the spacebar between two words that are not included inside a set of quotation marks. Using quotation marks around a phrase of any length causes the search engine to keep the phrase intact while looking for results. Not using quotation marks can result in a return of hits that are more indicative of having used Boolean logic, with the spaces between words acting as a hidden OR command.

The following examples illustrate two ways to use Boolean logic to limit search results in our scenario:

+"economic depression" +1930

+depression -illness -"art form"

SYNONYMS

A major challenge that students face when attempting to use search tools on the Internet is their limited vocabulary. This is particularly true for students whose primary language is not English and for young students. Once again, access to tools such as the thesaurus or assistance from a library or media specialist can provide students with techniques designed to increase the likelihood of a successful search.

Rather than searching for "economic depression," a student could try "Great Depression" or "economic crash" or "economic slump." By trying these various synonyms, new resources might be made available that would have been missed.

UPDATED TOOLS

Search tools are updated frequently. Using a variety of search tools and repeating searches after some time has passed may generate new, updated material for the researcher.

Multimedia Searches

Searching for specific forms of multimedia on the Internet is relatively easy. Many search engines provide links to video and audio files, as well as still images. For example, to locate a sound file for a speech given by President Kennedy concerning the Cuban Missile Crisis, a student might go to any one of the search engines, click on the link to "audio," and enter the appropriate search criteria. Try the following exercise to see how this might work.

1. Using the search engine All the Web, select the audio tab at the top of the screen.
2. Type "Kennedy" into the search window and click on search. The results will include any sound files that include the word Kennedy. These will not be restricted to John F. Kennedy.

SECTION 1—STRATEGIES FOR GETTING STARTED

A revision to the strategy can be made to include the single word "missile." This would more precisely target the desired results. A modified search phrase at All the Web reading +"John F. Kennedy" +missile would result in two sound files that would provide President Kennedy's speech on the Cuban Missile Crisis either in whole or in part. Changing the media type to video rather than audio would result in the actual video segment aired on national television on October 22, 1962. Imagine the effect on the student who is conducting research into this topic upon hearing or seeing President Kennedy as he delivered this speech.

Evaluating the Quality of the Resource

Students should be encouraged to access more than one search tool, including a combination of search engines, directories, and specialized databases, to ensure access to quality materials and resources. Once a resource is located, students should take the time to evaluate the quality of the information before they use it in their work. Encourage students to check for the following:

Accuracy. How reliable and free from error is the information?

Authority. What are the qualifications of the author who wrote the information?

Objectivity. Is the information presented with a minimum of bias?

Currency. Is the information up-to-date? How can you tell?

Coverage. Is the topic explored in depth?

Search Tool Resources

Academic Info: **www.academicinfo.net**
All the Web: **www.alltheweb.com**
AltaVista: **www.altavista.com**
American Memory Collection: **http://memory.loc.gov/ammem/**
California Digital Library SearchLight, Social Science and Humanities:
  http://searchlight.cdlib.org/cgi-bin/searchlight?SSH
Direct Search Campaign: **www.freepint.com/gary/campaign.htm**
DogPile: **www.dogpile.com**
The Educator's Reference Desk: **www.eduref.org**
ERIC Database: **www.eduref.org/Eric/**
Federal Resources for Educational Excellence:
  http://wdcrobcolp01.ed.gov/cfapps/free/displaysubject.cfm?sid=9
Google: **www.google.com**
The Historian's Sources:
  http://lcweb2.loc.gov/ammem/ndlpedu/lessons/psources/pshome.html
Historical Text Archive: **http://historicaltextarchive.com**
Historical Treasure Chests: **www.k12science.org/curriculum/treasure/**
Infomine: **http://infomine.ucr.edu**
InfoPlease: **www.infoplease.com**
Internet Public Library: **www.ipl.org**
The Invisible Web: **www.invisible-web.net**
iTools: **www.itools.com**
Librarian's Index to the Internet: **http://lii.org**

National Archives and Records Administration:
   www.archivcs.gov/digital_classroom/index.html
Political Cartoons: **http://cagle.slate.msn.com/teacher/middle/lessonplanMS4.asp**
Primary Sources on the Web:
   www.lib.berkeley.edu/TeachingLib/Guides/PrimarySourcesOnTheWeb.html
Refdesk: **www.refdesk.com**
Teoma: **www.teoma.com**
20th Century History Resources: **http://history1900s.about.com**
Vivisimo: **http://vivisimo.com**
Yahoo!: **www.yahoo.com**

chapter 4

WALTER MCKENZIE

Constructing a Rubric

As constructivist instructional practices have become part of the mainstream in education, assessment rubrics have gained in popularity. Teachers no longer teach the curriculum or teach the text; they teach the child. Their role is not to disseminate information but to support learners in building understandings. The rubric is an excellent tool for assessing student progress in this type of educational environment. It frees teachers from the limitations of traditional pencil and paper assessments and places the focus on student performance.

It sounds wonderful, but how does a teacher go about creating a rubric that will successfully measure student learning? There is a deliberate set of steps in designing an original rubric:

- State the lesson objective.
- Design an assessment task that allows the student to demonstrate his or her success in mastering the objective.
- Develop a set of observable, measurable criteria that can be used to evaluate the assessment task.
- Identify levels or degrees of success for the criteria.
- Craft statements that describe each level of success for each criterion.

Let's take a closer look at each step of the process.

State the Lesson Objective

As in any effective lesson, the instructional objective must be stated up front. It is the foundation on which the entire lesson is built, including the assessment. The objective should be stated in concrete terms, clearly identifying the task the learner will be asked to accomplish. Teachers are trained in the writing of objectives, and this becomes second nature as they gain experience in the classroom.

However, the challenge of the objective may not be in how it is stated, but in how it is crafted. If teachers simply state that given pencil and paper the student will complete an objective test on Greek and Roman forms of government with at least 70% accuracy, they will get exactly what they have asked for: rote recall of facts and figures to successfully fill in blanks. It's quick and it's easily measured, but does it really give an accurate idea of what students have learned? On the other hand, consider the ways students would demonstrate their understanding of early Western forms of government if the objective asked them to create a Venn diagram showing the similarities and differences between the Greek and Roman systems. Now students have to apply their knowledge to compare and contrast both systems of government.

SECTION 1—STRATEGIES FOR GETTING STARTED

Faced with the choice of these two assessment tasks, teachers have traditionally stuck with the objective test because there were not a lot of options available for accurately measuring student learning if there was more than one right answer. What if different students use different idioms for expressing their understanding? Doesn't it become hard to manage if there is no finite set of acceptable responses to the assessment task? And how do teachers quantify degrees of success when every student's Venn diagram can be so unique? The rubric can address all these questions. Most important, though, it invites teachers to craft assessment tasks that aren't looking for a single right answer. It allows students to perform at higher levels of thinking. The key is crafting assessment tasks that go beyond the objective to more open-ended, subjective activities.

Design an Assessment Task

Once you are satisfied you have an objective that allows for varied forms of student performance, you must craft an assessment task that will follow through on the intent of your objective. The single most common error teachers make in designing assessments is to create tasks that are not consistent with the lesson objective. For example, if students are to learn how to read the periodic table of the elements, it would be inconsistent to assess their understanding by asking students to create their own imaginary element, and present it in a colorful drawing. It would make a creative bulletin board display for Back to School night, but it would not measure the intended objective of the lesson: to accurately interpret the properties of the elements on the periodic table.

Rather, revisit the assessment task for measuring how accurately students can read and interpret the nomenclature on the periodic table by tweaking this creative idea. Yes, students can create original elements, but have them present their new discoveries by creating actual entries for the periodic table complete with symbols, atomic numbers, and all the details that make the table so useful. To extend the task, students could write a paragraph description of their new element, including how it was discovered, where it belongs on the periodic table, and what traits make it a new and unique element. In this way students can be imaginative while still being held to the standards set in the periodic table. If they can read and interpret one another's entries for new elements on the table, then they surely have mastered the prescribed skill in the objective.

Develop a Set of Observable, Measurable Criteria

With the objective and assessment task in place, the teacher is now ready to develop a list of criteria for assessing each student's work product. These criteria should be general enough to apply to a range of student products but specific enough that everyone can agree on their meaning. For the assessment task of creating and presenting an original element in the format of the periodic table, criteria might include:

- creation of an original symbol;
- indication of the atomic number;
- inclusion of the atomic weight;

- proper placement on the periodic table based on the element's characteristics; and
- a descriptive paragraph of at least five complete sentences that explains the origin and properties of this newfound element.

In addition, teachers may want to include other criteria on which they place emphasis in their classrooms. Such assessments might include whether the project is

- turned in on time;
- neat and clean in appearance;
- free of errors; or
- labeled with the proper heading.

This is the beauty of rubric construction. You decide which values to emphasize in evaluating student work.

For each of these examples, the criterion is succinctly stated, observable, and measurable in student work. Writing a concise set of criteria will take some soul-searching as you decide what you truly want to stress in assessing student work. But once you realize your priorities for learning, you will find the process highly rewarding for both you and your students.

Identify Degrees of Success for the Criteria

With your criteria in place, you are now ready to determine the degrees of success you want to establish for student work. A three-point rubric is always popular because it provides for basic levels of success: unsatisfactory, satisfactory, and exemplary. Then again, a four-point scale gives your rubric a greater sensitivity to degrees of student success: unsatisfactory, satisfactory, exemplary, and exceptional. The more levels you build in, the more sophisticated your rubric will be. If you want a quick and easy assessment tool, a three-point scale may suffice. Then again, if you're assessing major projects at the end of a unit, you may choose to develop a five-point scale that provides finer distinctions among degrees of success.

SECTION 1—STRATEGIES FOR GETTING STARTED

For the periodic table rubric, I will select a three-point scale. I don't want to go into great detail because it is not a summative assessment. It would look like the following example.

Periodic Table Rubric

EXAMPLE RUBRIC

CRITERIA	1 UNSATISFACTORY	2 SATISFACTORY	3 EXEMPLARY
Creation of an original symbol			
Indication of the atomic number			
Inclusion of the atomic weight			
Proper placement on the periodic table based on the element's characteristics			
A descriptive paragraph of at least five complete sentences that explains the origin and properties of this newfound element			

With the criteria and levels of success in place, we are ready for the final step in creating our rubric.

Craft Exemplars for Each Criterion

What truly makes the rubric an effective assessment tool are the exemplars, or descriptors of success, for each criterion. In the previous example, the rubric is still incomplete. Any teacher can arbitrarily assign points to a student work product based on his or her own subjective values. To make the rubric a truly objective instrument, exemplars are a must. Exemplars descriptively state the degrees of success for each criterion that both the teacher and students can understand. Consider the first criterion in the following example:

Periodic Table Rubric

EXAMPLE RUBRIC EXCERPT

CRITERIA	1 UNSATISFACTORY	2 SATISFACTORY	3 EXEMPLARY
	No symbol is evident or the symbol offered does not follow the conventions of the periodic table.	A symbol is offered that is consistent with the conventions of the periodic table.	A symbol is offered that is consistent with the conventions of the periodic table and reveals personality traits unique to this student.

CHAPTER 4—CONSTRUCTING A RUBRIC

Exemplars are critical in filling out a rubric that offers meaningful feedback to students and parents. Once you have a rubric in place, you may choose to share it with your students before they begin their assessment task so that they will know the standards they are working to meet and exceed. In this way it becomes more than just another assessment tool. Your rubric actually becomes a key component in your instruction.

After teachers have modeled several rubrics themselves in the course of the school year, they may choose to engage their students in a discussion of the criteria that should be included in assessing student work, actually building rubrics together. This takes constructivist teaching to an entirely new height, with students sharing in the responsibility for developing assessments and thereby taking a greater ownership in their own learning. Moreover, actively involving students in rubric construction helps instill in them the high standards they need to set for themselves. Properly constructed rubrics can make all this happen for you in your classroom.

section 2

Resource Units

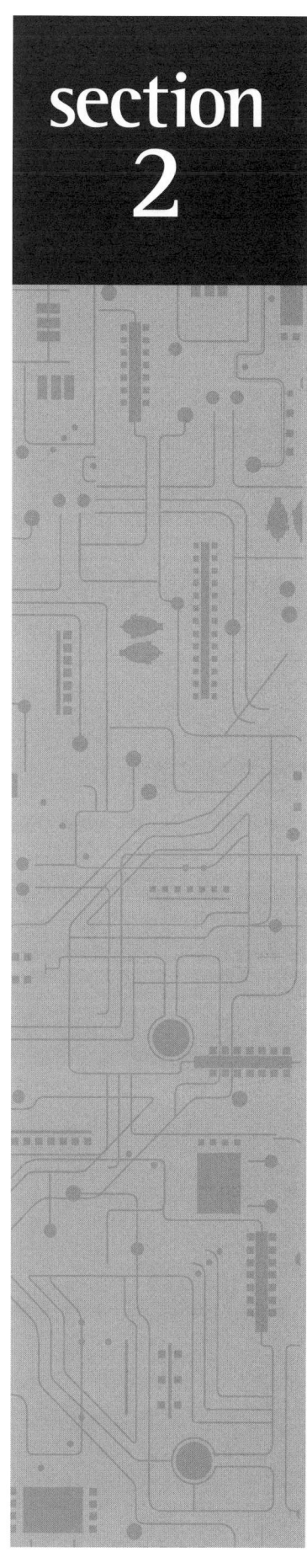

The Seven Pillars of the Constitution
Mathew Manweller

A Flash Tapestry: A Digital Study of the Battle of Hastings
Walter McKenzie

The Civil War: A Multimedia Investigation
Michael Hutchison

Money, Special Interest Groups, and Reelection Rates
Mathew Manweller

Gross Domestic Product and World Events
Donna Archibald

How Social Are We Anyway?
Cyndy Jones Woods

Virtual Reality, Cultural Reality: A Study of the Middle East
Walter McKenzie

Political Polling: Measuring Support for Environmental Policies
Mathew Manweller

The Modern Presidency
Michael Hutchison

All the World in an Archipelago
Cyndy Jones Woods

Many Shades Are We: An Examination of the Diverse Cultures That Make Up America
Donna Archibald

From *Plessy* to *Brown*: Concept Mapping the U.S. Supreme Court
Mathew Manweller

Prisoner's Dilemma: A Wireless Simulation of the Romanov Court
Walter McKenzie

Scene at the Signing of the Constitution of the United States, by Howard Chandler Christy. This painting hangs in the east stairway in the House wing of the United States Capitol.

The Seven Pillars of the Constitution

MATHEW MANWELLER

"It is the genius of our Constitution that under its shelter of enduring institutions and rooted principles there is ample room for the rich fertility of American political invention."

President Lyndon Johnson

UNIT OBJECTIVES

Students will be challenged to:

- Examine and differentiate the different political and structural principles embedded within the U.S. Constitution.

- Collaborate electronically with other students to classify constitutional clauses.

- Investigate the principles of federalism, popular sovereignty, checks and balances, separation of powers, judicial review, limited government, and flexibility.

- Use software to organize, classify, and present findings.

SOCIAL STUDIES STANDARDS ADDRESSED

V Individuals, Groups, and Institutions
Social studies programs should include experiences that provide for the study of interactions among individuals, groups, and institutions.

VI Power, Authority, and Governance
Social studies programs should include experiences that provide for the study of how people create and change structures of power, authority, and governance.

X Civic Ideals and Practices
Social studies programs should include experiences that provide for the study of the ideals, principles, and practices of citizenship in a democratic republic.

NETS•S ADDRESSED

3 Technology Productivity Tools
- Students use technology tools to enhance learning, increase productivity, and promote creativity.
- Students use productivity tools to collaborate in constructing technology-enhanced models, preparing publications, and producing other creative works.

4 Technology Communications Tools
- Students use telecommunications to collaborate, publish, and interact with peers, experts, and other audiences.
- Students use a variety of media and formats to communicate information and ideas effectively to multiple audiences.

6 Technology Problem-Solving and Decision-Making Tools
- Students use technology resources for solving problems and making informed decisions.
- Students employ technology in the development of strategies for solving problems in the real world.

CENTRAL DISCIPLINE AREA

The U.S. Constitution

The study of the Constitution is central to most American government classes. As the nation's founding document, it provides the structure and guiding principles for all laws at the federal and state level. Any understanding of American government starts with an understanding of the Constitution. This unit will challenge students to study each of the principles embedded within the Constitution and use technology to disassemble and analyze the document clause by clause.

UNIT DESCRIPTION

It is generally accepted by scholars that the Constitution reflects seven basic political principles: federalism, popular sovereignty, checks and balances, separation of powers, judicial review, limited government, and flexibility. One way to illustrate this concept to students is to have them "dissect" or "disassemble" the Constitution clause by clause.

In this unit students will study the seven principles, examining each of the clauses in the Constitution (or a subset of clauses selected by the teacher), and decide which principle the clause reflects. For example, Article 1, Clause 2, of the Constitution indicates election of the House by popular vote. This clause would fall under the category of popular sovereignty. As a more complicated example, Article 1, Section 4, explains how states set the times, places, and manner of holding elections, but the Congress may alter such regulations. This clause illustrates federalism.

Students will download a copy of the U.S. Constitution into a word processing file. In a separate document they will create a seven-column chart or table, with each column corresponding to one of the seven principles. Students will then copy clauses from the Constitution and paste them into the appropriate column. Because the Constitution is vague in some places, there will be disagreements over the classification of some clauses. To rectify this, students will solicit feedback on their documents by posting to an online discussion board, by generating a communal e-mail debate through Yahoo! Groups, or by beaming the charts directly using handheld computers. When students receive other documents, they will use the Track Changes feature in Word to suggest alternative classification options.

Unit Tools

INTERDISCIPLINARY LINKS

U.S. and World History: The Constitution is more than 200 years old. In order for students to understand many of its clauses and principles, they will need to understand the backdrop in which the Constitution was drafted. For example, students will need to develop a solid understanding of *Marbury* v. *Madison*, the Magna Charta, and historical terms such as *capitation taxes*.

Law: The Constitution also contains many legal terms with which students will not be familiar. Either through lecture or Internet research, students will need to learn about terms such as *bill of attainder*, *ex post facto law*, *due process*, and *eminent domain*.

THE TRACK CHANGES FEATURE

Microsoft Word and other quality word processing programs offer a handy way to keep track of changes made to a document. Versions of MS Word vary, but in most, go to the Tools menu, choose the Track Changes submenu, then select Highlight Changes. Now, when someone else makes changes to the document, Word will indicate the changes with revision marks. After the document is reviewed, you can see the changes made by the different reviewers because each reviewer's changes will be marked with a different color. After viewing tracked changes, you can accept or reject each change. You can also choose to show or hide tracked changes on the screen or in the printed document by using the Highlight Changes dialog box.

SECTION 2—RESOURCE UNITS

SPOTLIGHT ON TECHNOLOGY

Internet Research: As students examine the Constitution, they will encounter terms that are unfamiliar. Students may use the Internet to research these terms.

Word Processing: Word processors can be used for more than simply writing essays and reports. They can be used to create tables and charts, cut and paste writing from other documents, and highlight important information within a document. In this unit, students will use word processing software to organize a classification scheme and present their projects to other students and the instructor.

Asynchronous Communication: Any classification process is subjective. As a result, the class will need to deliberate over how certain constitutional clauses should be classified. Deliberation may take place using Blackboard, Yahoo! Groups, TappedIn, or some other virtual discussion medium. For instance, students may solicit and offer peer review feedback by posting the first drafts of their project to a virtual discussion board such as Blackboard and commenting on the work of others. They may also use Yahoo! Groups to send and receive communal e-mails.

Handheld Devices: In schools with more advanced technology capabilities, students can use handheld computers to send and receive feedback.

TECHNOLOGY RESOURCES NEEDED

Hardware
computers with Internet access
handheld computers (optional)

Software
Internet browsing software
word processing software
e-mail software
semantic mapping software (optional)

WEB AND LITERATURE RESOURCES

Web Resources
All Experts (Constitution questions):
    www.allexperts.com/getExpert.asp?Category=340
Ask an Expert: **www.askanexpert.com**
Ask Jeeves: **www.ask.com**
Blackboard: **http://company.blackboard.com**
Congresslink (Constitution with links to definitions):
    www.congresslink.org/resourc.html
Constitution Community:
    www.archives.gov/digital_classroom/constitution_community.html
Constitution Online: **www.usconstitution.net**
The Constitution (WebQuest):
    www.greece.k12.ny.us/oly/techprep/webquest/constitution.html
Discovery.com WebQuests:
    http://school.discovery.com/schrockguide/webquest/webquest.html
Documents From the Continental Congress and the Constitutional Convention, 1774–1789: **http://memory.loc.gov/ammem/bdsds/bdsdhome.html**
Federalist Papers: **http://lcWeb2.loc.gov/const/fed/fedpapers.html**

Federalist Papers Search: www.law.emory.edu/FEDERAL/federalist/federser.html
Index of Constitutional Provisions: http://press-pubs.uchicago.edu/founders/indexes/constitutional_provisions_index.html
Law.Com Dictionary: http://dictionary.law.com
Law for Kids: www.lawforkids.org/LawDocs/Constitution.cfm
Library of Congress (copy of Constitution): http://memory.loc.gov/const/const.html
Magna Carta: http://www.bl.uk/collections/treasures/magna.html
National Constitution Center: www.constitutioncenter.org/explore/TheU.S.Constitution/index.shtml
Some Thoughts About WebQuests (Bernie Dodge): http://faculty.fullerton.edu/tgreen/constitution/teacher.htm
TappedIn: http://ti2.sri.com/tappedin/
The U.S. Constitution: http://projects.edtech.sandi.net/marston/constitution/
We Were There: WebQuest on the U.S. Constitutional Convention: http://babylon.k12.ny.us/usconstitution/
Yahoo! Groups: http://groups.yahoo.com

Literature Resources

The American Constitution: Its Origins and Development, Alfred Kelly, Winfred Harbison, & Herman Belz

Black's Law Dictionary, Bryan A. Garner (Ed.)

A Brilliant Solution: Inventing the American Constitution, Carol Berkin

The Debate on the Constitution: Federalist and Antifederalist Speeches, Articles, and Letters During the Struggle Over Ratification, Part Two: January to August 1788, Bernard Bailyn (Ed.)

Declaring Rights: A Brief History With Documents, Jack Rakove

The Living U.S. Constitution, Saul K. Padover & Jacob W. Landynski

Miracle at Philadelphia: The Story of the Constitutional Convention, May to September 1787, Catherine Drinker Bowen

Original Meanings: Politics and Ideas in the Making of the Constitution, Jack N. Rakove

The Origins of the American Constitution: A Documentary History, Michael Kammen

Our Constitution: The Myth That Binds Us, Eric Black

Understanding the U.S. Constitution, Mark Stange

What Kind of Nation: Thomas Jefferson, John Marshall, and the Epic Struggle to Create a United States, James F. Simon

The Words We Live By: Your Annotated Guide to the Constitution, Linda Monk

SECTION 2—RESOURCE UNITS

DAYS 1–3   Students need to gain an understanding of the seven principles (noted in the Unit Description) that pervade the Constitution. Teachers can use lectures, textbooks, or Internet research to accomplish this task. Depending on the desired depth of understanding, this will take from one to three days. For teachers using the Internet, a WebQuest would be an effective way for students to gain the knowledge.

The following three WebQuests were created by teachers. You may want to incorporate them into your lesson as is or use them as a model for creating your own.

- **www.greece.k12.ny.us/oly/techprep/webquest/constitution.html**
- **http://projects.edtech.sandi.net/roosevelt/constitution/**
- **http://babylon.k12.ny.us/usconstitution/**

DAY 4   Students need to access a copy of the U.S. Constitution at any of the provided Web sites (see the Web Resources section). Instruct them to copy and paste the text into a Word file. After saving the file, have them open a second blank Word document and, using the Table menu, create a seven-column chart like in Figure 1.

FIGURE 1. A word processing table helps students examine the Constitution.

Federalism	Popular Sovereignty	Checks and Balances	Separation of Powers	Limited Government	Flexibility	Judicial Review

It is helpful to switch the page alignment in the word processing software to "landscape." This will allow the entire chart to fit on the page. The rows will automatically expand as students input text.

DAYS 5–6   Working independently, or in groups if the teacher prefers, students begin examining the individual clauses in the Constitution (or the subset selected by the teacher). After reading the clause and deciding which political principle it illustrates, they should cut and paste the clause into the correct table column.

The following are important notes about this stage of the unit:

- Some clauses will not fit into any of the seven options. For example, Article I, Section 2, Paragraph 3, indicates members of the House of Representatives must be at least 25 years old. This is simply a procedural requirement and illustrates none of the seven principles. Students should be informed that some clauses fit nowhere.

- Judicial review was not established until 16 years after the ratification of the Constitution with the decision of *Marbury v. Madison* (1803). Therefore, students will not find any clauses relating to judicial review. As the teacher, you may want to tell your students or you may choose to allow them to discover this fact on their own.

- Some clauses may legitimately fit into more than one category. For example, Article V describes how the Constitution can be amended, noting that the House and Senate must pass an amendment by a 2/3 vote in each body and then 3/4 of the states must also ratify the amendment. Therefore, Article V could be placed in the flexibility column or the federalism column.

DAYS 7–8 After disassembling the Constitution into a table, students should post their work to Blackboard or use one of the asynchronous communication Web sites to disseminate their work to classmates. Blackboard will allow students to debate how specific clauses should be classified. Or, using Yahoo! Groups, a debate could take place through a series of communal e-mails. One option is to have students download some of the documents they received and offer feedback. This should be done using the Track Changes feature of Word. Students can insert color-coded comments, informing fellow students why they feel a certain clause should be placed elsewhere. Or, they can simply cut and paste the document to reflect their ideas. The Track Changes feature will highlight from where, and to where, all the text has been moved. When they are done editing classmates' documents, the projects should be reposted. The teacher may want use some technique to ensure everyone gets some feedback, perhaps three reviews for each student.

DAY 9 Students retrieve their peer-reviewed documents. After reading each copy and assessing the validity of the comments, students can then "accept" or "reject" the proposed changes to their document. They should conclude by finalizing one document they will turn in to the teacher to be graded.

DAY 10 (OPTIONAL) Teachers may want students to justify or explain why they have placed certain clauses where they have. This can be done using footnotes. (In Word, look under the Insert menu for Reference, Annotation, or Footnotes.) Students simply place the cursor at the end of the text, and add a reference. A number will appear at the bottom of the page and students can then type their justification (Figure 2).

TEACHING TIPS Take some time to let students explore how their word processor works. Let them practice making different tables, using footnotes, and experimenting with the Track Changes feature.

FIGURE 2. Students can explain their choices using footnotes.

Federalism	Popular Sovereignty	Checks and Balances	Separation of Powers	Limited Government	Flexibility	Judicial Review
Article 1, Section 3. The Senate of the United States shall be composed of two Senators from each state, chosen by the legislature thereof.[1]	Article 1, Section 2. The House of Representatives shall be composed of members chosen every second year by the people of the several states.[2]	Article 1, Section 7. Every bill which shall have passed the House of Representatives and the Senate, shall, before it become a law, be presented to the President of the United States; if he approve he shall sign it.	Article 1, Section 1. All legislative powers herein granted shall be vested in a Congress of the United States, which shall consist of a Senate and House of Representatives.	Article 1, Section 9. No bill of attainder or ex post facto Law shall be passed.	Article 1, Section 8. To make all laws which shall be necessary and proper for carrying into execution the foregoing powers, and all other powers vested by this Constitution in the government of the United States, or in any department or officer thereof.	

[1] Because the state legislatures get to decide who will serve in the federal Senate, this is federalism.
[2] Because the people are electing the House member directly, this is popular sovereignty.

Complete a few classifications as a class. Use a projection device on your computer and cut and paste a few constitutional clauses into a sample table you have created. This will give students some practice before they begin.

LESSON EXTENDERS

Have students repeat the project, but use a different document such as the Declaration of Independence or some of the Federalist Papers.

Lead a class discussion. Examine the clauses in which students could not reach a consensus concerning the column to which the item should be assigned. Use an Internet "ask an expert" Web site to be the arbitrator.

Find an American government teacher in another school with whom to collaborate. Set up a videoconferencing day for the classes to compare conclusions. Or, simply expand the e-mail or virtual discussion board part of this unit to include students from another school.

Use semantic mapping software to visually demonstrate student understanding of the relationships among the seven pillars.

Assessment

CRITERIA	1 UNSATISFACTORY	2 SATISFACTORY	3 EXEMPLARY	SCORE
SOCIAL STUDIES STANDARDS				
Understanding of interactions among individuals, groups, and institutions	Understanding is not in evidence.	Student demonstrates acceptable understanding within the context of this project.	Student demonstrates exemplary understanding, making connections to personal experience through higher level applications of thinking.	
Recognition that people create and change structures of power, authority, and governance	Understanding is not in evidence.	Student demonstrates acceptable understanding within the context of this project.	Student demonstrates exemplary understanding, making connections to personal experience through higher level applications of thinking.	
Understanding of the ideals, principles, and practices of citizenship in a democratic republic	Understanding is not in evidence.	Student demonstrates acceptable understanding within the context of this project.	Student demonstrates exemplary understanding, making connections to personal experience through higher level applications of thinking.	
NETS				
Use of technology productivity tools	Student shows lack of minimum proficiency in using these tools.	Student meets minimum proficiency for using these tools.	Student goes beyond minimum proficiency for using these tools, applying their use beyond the requirements of this project.	
Use of technology communications tools	Student shows lack of minimum proficiency in using these tools.	Student meets minimum proficiency for using these tools.	Student goes beyond minimum proficiency for using these tools, applying their use beyond the requirements of this project.	
Use of technology problem-solving and decision-making tools	Student shows lack of minimum proficiency in using these tools.	Student meets minimum proficiency for using these tools.	Student goes beyond minimum proficiency for using these tools, applying their use beyond the requirements of this project.	
			Subtotal Points	

continued next page

Assessment

CRITERIA	1 UNSATISFACTORY	2 SATISFACTORY	3 EXEMPLARY	SCORE
TABLE				
Completeness of table	Table has four or fewer categories completed or fewer than three entries in at least two columns.	Table has five categories completed or fewer than three entries in one column.	Table has all six categories completed with at least five entries in each column.	
Accuracy of table	There are two or more incorrect clauses placed in each column or a total of 12 incorrectly placed clauses.	There is one incorrect clause in each column or a total of six incorrectly placed clauses.	There are fewer than six incorrectly placed clauses in the entire chart.	
Quality of peer review feedback	Student offers no helpful suggestions to partner or the suggestions are inaccurate.	Student offers a few suggestions and they are mostly accurate.	Student offers several insightful suggestions.	
Quality of references	Student does not use footnotes to explain any entries, or the student has more than 10 inaccurate explanations.	Student uses footnotes on at least half the entries, and has fewer than 10 inaccurate explanations.	Student uses footnotes to explain every entry, and fewer than five explanations are inaccurate.	
			Total Points	

A section of the Bayeux Tapestry, which depicts the Battle of Hastings.

A Flash Tapestry: A Digital Study of the Battle of Hastings

WALTER MCKENZIE

"An invasion of armies can be resisted, but not an idea whose time has come."

Victor Hugo

UNIT OBJECTIVES

Students will be challenged to:

- Determine the timeline of activity revealed in the Bayeux Tapestry.

- Compare the events in the Bayeux Tapestry with other historical accounts of the Battle of Hastings.

- Build consensus on an accurate account of the battle.

- Create icons that represent key persons and events in the battle.

- Import the icons into a Flash movie and convert them to buttons.

- Associate links from each button that can be accessed when viewing an original Flash movie of the Battle of Hastings.

SECTION 2—RESOURCE UNITS

SOCIAL STUDIES STANDARDS ADDRESSED

V   **Individuals, Groups, and Institutions**
Social studies programs should include experiences that provide for the study of interactions among individuals, groups, and institutions.

VIII   **Science, Technology, and Society**
Social studies programs should include experiences that provide for the study of relationships among science, technology, and society.

X   **Civic Ideals and Practices**
Social studies programs should include experiences that provide for the study of the ideals, principles, and practices of citizenship in a democratic republic.

NETS•S ADDRESSED

3   **Technology Productivity Tools**
- Students use productivity tools to collaborate in constructing technology-enhanced models, preparing publications, and producing other creative works.

4   **Technology Communications Tools**
- Students use a variety of media and formats to communicate information and ideas effectively to multiple audiences.

5   **Technology Research Tools**
- Students use technology to locate, evaluate, and collect information from a variety of sources.
- Students use technology tools to process data and report results.
- Students evaluate and select new information resources and technological innovations based on the appropriateness to specific tasks.

6   **Technology Problem-Solving and Decision-Making Tools**
- Students employ technology in the development of strategies for solving problems in the real world.

CENTRAL DISCIPLINE AREA

Historiography

Access to the World Wide Web in the classroom has allowed students to examine many historical documents heretofore unavailable. With this recent explosion in primary and secondary sources, students have the opportunity to practice historiography to evaluate various sources and synthesize findings into a meaningful, modern digital work product. This process promotes higher order thinking and information literacy skills, which are so critical to be contributing participants in the 21st-century age of information.

A FLASH TAPESTRY: A DIGITAL STUDY OF THE BATTLE OF HASTINGS

UNIT DESCRIPTION — The Norman invasion of England in 1066 serves as the starting point for the modern English state. While the Bayeux Tapestry has been long considered a significant primary source in understanding the events of October 14, 1066, other primary sources recorded for the ages also help to provide a composite picture of the actual events. Students will examine sources in an electronic format and develop their own understanding of the Battle of Hastings by creating an interactive Flash movie.

Unit Tools

INTERDISCIPLINARY LINKS

Language Arts: Students will read and analyze primary source documents to corroborate events at the Battle of Hastings and identify a plausible storyline. Students will then storyboard their battle timeline in preparation for creating a Flash movie. Students will also create HTML documents that serve as local links from the Flash movie, explaining significant persons and events from the battle.

Information Literacy: Students will analyze primary and secondary sources for validity and accuracy.

SPOTLIGHT ON TECHNOLOGY

Internet Research: Students will use the Web to access and analyze primary and secondary sources.

Graphics Editing: Students will create original icons in GIF format that represent specific persons and events for their Flash movie.

HTML Editing: Students will create text-based Web pages that are launched from Flash movie icons to explain specific elements of the battle.

Flash: Students will create a Flash movie consisting of animated buttons and local links that explain their understanding of the battle.

TECHNOLOGY RESOURCES NEEDED

Hardware
- computers with Internet access
- digital scanner

Software
- Web browser
- word processor
- graphics editor
- HTML editor
- Flash

WEB, LITERATURE, AND CD RESOURCES

Web Resources
- Anglo Saxon Britain, Viking Raids and the Norman Invasion: **www.great-britain.co.uk/history/ang-sax.htm**
- Battle of Fulford: **www.battleoffulford.org.uk/**

SECTION 2—RESOURCE UNITS

Battle of Hastings:
   www.bbc.co.uk/history/games/hastings/about/hastings2.shtml
Battle of Hastings: 1066: **www.battle1066.com**
Bayeux Tapestry: **www.angelfire.com/rnb/bayeux_tapestry/index.html**
Bayeux Tapestry: **www.ealdormere.sca.org/university/bayeux.shtml**
Bayeux Tapestry Digital Edition:
   www.essentialnormanconquest.com/osehnctapestry.html
Historic Tale Construction Kit: **www.adgame-wonderland.de/type/bayeux.php**
Invasion of England: 1066: **www.eyewitnesstohistory.com/bayeux.htm**
Norman Conquest School Site: **www.normanconquest.co.uk/three_kings.htm**
Normans: **www.wsu.edu:8080/~dee/MA/NORMANS.HTM**
Reading the Bayeux Tapestry: **www.bayeuxtapestry.org.uk/**
Secrets of the Norman Invasion: **www.secretsofthenormaninvasion.com**
Synopsis of the Battle of Hastings: **www.infokey.com/hon/hastings.htm**
1066: A Medieval Mosaic: **www.1066.co.nz**
1066: The Events of the Norman Conquest:
   www.geocities.com/Athens/Aegean/3532/1066.htm
Threat of Invasion 1066–1789: An Overview:
   www.bbc.co.uk/history/war/invasion_threat_01.shtml

Literature Resources
   The Anglo-Saxon Chronicle, Michael Swanton (Ed.)
   The Anglo-Saxons, James Campbell
   The Battle of Hastings, Jim Bradbury
   The Bayeux Tapestry, David M. Wilson
   The Bayeux Tapestry: Monument to a Norman Triumph, Wolfgang Grape
   The Bayeux Tapestry; The Story of the Norman Conquest: 1066, Norman George
   Harold: The Last Anglo-Saxon King, Ian W. Walker
   Invitation to Old English and Anglo-Saxon England, Bruce Mitchell
   The Rhetoric of Power in the Bayeux Tapestry, Suzanne Lewis
   1066: The Year of the Conquest, David Howarth
   William the Conqueror: The Norman Impact Upon England, David C. Douglas
   The Year 1000: What Life Was Like at the Turn of the First Millennium, Danny
      Robert & Danziger Lacey

CD-ROM
   The Bayeux Tapestry on CD-ROM, Martin K. Foys

A FLASH TAPESTRY: A DIGITAL STUDY OF THE BATTLE OF HASTINGS

teaching the unit

DAY 1 Group students into teams of four or five and have them study the Battle of Hastings. Assign each group a specific section to study at **www.battle1066.com**: Vikings, Normans, Saxons, Harold of Wessex, William of Normandy, and the Bayeux Tapestry. Ask each group to research their specific assignment and take notes on significant information.

DAY 2 Assign each group additional text and Web-based resources to gather more information with the requirement that any fact to be included in their research must be corroborated by a second independent source.

DAY 3 Have the same groups work separately examining the following Web-based resources concerning the Bayeux Tapestry:

> Bayeux Tapestry: **www.angelfire.com/rnb/bayeux_tapestry/index.html**
> Bayeux Tapestry: **www.ealdormere.sca.org/university/bayeux.shtml**
> Bayeux Tapestry Digital Edition:
>   **www.essentialnormanconquest.com/osehnctapestry.html**
> Historic Tale Construction Kit: **www.adgame-wonderland.de/type/bayeux.php**
> Invasion of England: 1066: **www.eyewitnesstohistory.com/bayeux.htm**
> Reading the Bayeux Tapestry: **www.bayeuxtapestry.org.uk/**

Ask each group to identify persons and events from their reading of the tapestry.

DAY 4 Use the following Internet resources (and any additional text or multimedia resources you have at hand) to corroborate the role of persons and accuracy of events that occurred at the Battle of Hastings.

> Battle of Hastings:
>   **www.bbc.co.uk/history/games/hastings/about/hastings2.shtml**
> Norman Conquest School Site: **www.normanconquest.co.uk/three_kings.htm**
> Secrets of the Norman Invasion: **www.secretsofthenormaninvasion.com**
> Synopsis of the Battle of Hastings: **www.infokey.com/hon/hastings.htm**
> 1066: A Medieval Mosaic: **www.1066.co.nz**
> 1066: The Events of the Norman Conquest:
>   **www.geocities.com/Athens/Aegean/3532/1066.htm**
> Threat of Invasion 1066–1789: An Overview:
>   **www.bbc.co.uk/history/war/invasion_threat_01.shtml**

Ask students to take notes on research that corroborates or contradicts the Bayeux Tapestry.

SECTION 2—RESOURCE UNITS

DAYS 5–6 Bring the class back together and come to a consensus on the major people and events of the Battle of Hastings. Work as a group to create a storyboard that presents the facts of the battle in a sequential timeline. Post the storyboard on a classroom wall for easy reference.

DAYS 7–12 Have students work in one of the following three groups:

- Students use a graphics editor to design icons that represent significant people and events in the Battle of Hastings. Instruct them to create the icons using a consistent scale of size and save them individually in GIF format.
- Students use an HTML editor to type original explanations of major people and events of the battle, based on class research. Direct students to save each event and person as an individual HTML file using an agreed-upon naming convention.
- Students use Flash to set up a movie for each frame in the class storyboard, complete with a standard background and border, a title page, and an index page. Instruct students to link each line on the index page to a separate Flash movie based on the storyboard and to be sure each individual Flash movie is named using a consistent pattern.

Circulate among each group and offer support and input as needed. All files should be saved in a common shared folder where everyone has access to them.

DAYS 13–19 Students work in groups on individual Flash movies from different parts of the class storyboard, importing icons, converting them to buttons, and creating links from their buttons to the HTML documents already created. On the 19th day have each group insert a Get URL link from their Flash movie to the next Flash movie in the sequence of the storyboard.

DAY 20 Publish each Flash movie as an HTML document and upload the entire set of files to your school server. Bring the class together to view the entire presentation of the battle in the succession of Flash movies they have created. Share the URL for viewing the presentation online.

TEACHING TIPS You should already have basic classroom management established in your classroom before attempting a project of this skill level.

Knowledge of graphics editing, HTML editing, and basic Flash construction is important in supporting your students in this unit. To brush up on a specific application you use for graphics, Web pages, or Flash, simply search using your favorite engine for tutorials on your products.

A FLASH TAPESTRY: A DIGITAL STUDY OF THE BATTLE OF HASTINGS

LESSON EXTENDERS

Have students create a credits page and a links page to supplement your Flash presentation of the battle online. Create a link from your school's main page to your Flash presentation.

Use student skills in creating digital graphics, Web pages, and Flash movies for new experiences in researching and understanding primary sources.

Assessment

CRITERIA	1 UNSATISFACTORY	2 SATISFACTORY	3 EXEMPLARY	SCORE
SOCIAL STUDIES STANDARDS				
Understanding of interactions among individuals, groups, and institutions	Understanding is not in evidence.	Student demonstrates acceptable understanding within the context of this project.	Student demonstrates exemplary understanding, making connections to personal experience through higher level applications of thinking.	
Understanding of relationships among science, technology, and society	Understanding is not in evidence.	Student demonstrates acceptable understanding within the context of this project.	Student demonstrates exemplary understanding, making connections to personal experience through higher level applications of thinking.	
Recognition of the ideals, principles, and practices of citizenship in a democratic republic	Understanding is not in evidence.	Student demonstrates acceptable understanding within the context of this project.	Student demonstrates exemplary understanding, making connections to personal experience through higher level applications of thinking.	
NETS				
Use of technology productivity tools	Student shows lack of minimum proficiency in using these tools.	Student meets minimum proficiency for using these tools.	Student goes beyond minimum proficiency for using these tools, applying their use beyond the requirements of this project.	
Use of technology communications tools	Student shows lack of minimum proficiency in using these tools.	Student meets minimum proficiency for using these tools.	Student goes beyond minimum proficiency for using these tools, applying their use beyond the requirements of this project.	
Use of technology research tools	Student shows lack of minimum proficiency in using these tools.	Student meets minimum proficiency for using these tools.	Student goes beyond minimum proficiency for using these tools, applying their use beyond the requirements of this project.	
Use of technology problem-solving and decision-making tools	Student shows lack of minimum proficiency in using these tools.	Student meets minimum proficiency for using these tools.	Student goes beyond minimum proficiency for using these tools, applying their use beyond the requirements of this project.	
			Subtotal Points	

continued next page

Assessment

CRITERIA	1 UNSATISFACTORY	2 SATISFACTORY	3 EXEMPLARY	SCORE
OTHER CLASS WORK				
Research content and quality	Information is not independently corroborated.	Information is corroborated by at least one independent source.	Information is corroborated by two or more independent sources.	
Concepts and understanding	Final work product does not demonstrate understanding of the Battle of Hastings.	Final work product demonstrates working understanding of the Battle of Hastings.	Final work product demonstrates working understanding of the Battle of Hastings and the process of historiography.	
Collaboration and participation	Student did not contribute as an active group member.	Student contributed as an active group member.	Student served as a leader for the group.	
			Total Points	

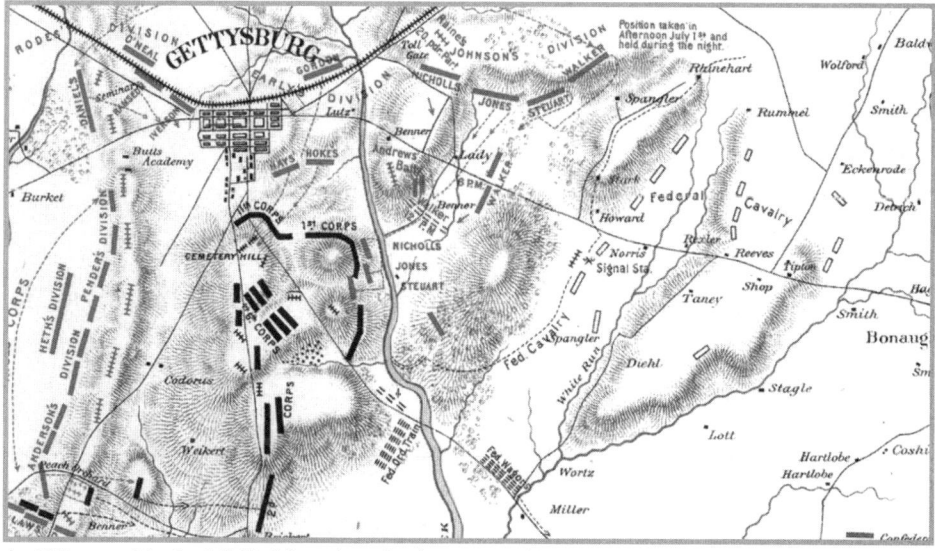

An 1863 map of the Battlefield of Gettysburg showing troop positions.

The Civil War: A Multimedia Investigation

MICHAEL HUTCHISON

"Fellow citizens, we cannot escape history ... The fiery trial through which we pass, will light us down, in honor or dishonor, to the latest generation."

Abraham Lincoln, 1862

UNIT OBJECTIVES

Students will be challenged to:

- Investigate various aspects of historical research and interpretation.

- Demonstrate competency in the use of computer technology.

- Develop an appreciation for the craftsmanship of historical research and investigation.

- Use software, digital video, and Internet resources to collect, analyze, and report information.

- Compare and contrast views of the Union and Confederate sides during the American Civil War.

SECTION 2—RESOURCE UNITS

SOCIAL STUDIES STANDARDS ADDRESSED

II Time, Continuity, and Change
Social studies programs should include experiences that provide for the study of the ways human beings view themselves in and over time.

VI Power, Authority, and Governance
Social studies programs should include experiences that provide for the study of how people create and change structures of power, authority, and governance.

X Civic Ideals and Practices
Social studies programs should include experiences that provide for the study of the ideals, principles, and practices of citizenship in a democratic republic.

NETS•S ADDRESSED

2 Social, Ethical, and Human Issues
- Students understand the ethical, cultural, and societal issues related to technology.
- Students practice responsible use of technology systems, information, and software.
- Students develop positive attitudes toward technology uses that support lifelong learning, collaboration, personal pursuits, and productivity.

3 Technology Productivity Tools
- Students use technology tools to enhance learning, increase productivity, and promote creativity.
- Students use productivity tools to collaborate in constructing technology-enhanced models, preparing publications, and producing other creative works.

5 Technology Research Tools
- Students use technology to locate, evaluate, and collect information from a variety of sources.
- Students use technology tools to process data and report results.
- Students evaluate and select new information resources and technological innovations based on the appropriateness to specific tasks.

THE CIVIL WAR: A MULTIMEDIA INVESTIGATION

CENTRAL DISCIPLINE AREA

United States Historiography

While many students *study* history, many are unaware of how history is written. Various interpretations of historic events sometimes skew students' viewpoints. Recent historical documentary films, such as *The Civil War* by Ken Burns, have increased public interest in that historic period, and feature films such as *Gettysburg* and *Gods and Generals* have also inspired interest in that era. The purpose of this lesson is twofold. Teachers of students who are studying the American Civil War may use this lesson in U.S. history classes. Teachers of students in history methods classes or general social studies classes may use this lesson as an exercise in how historians (and documentary filmmakers) write about historical events.

UNIT DESCRIPTION

The Civil War was a watershed event in U.S. history and, in the view of many historians, made the United States into a whole nation. In this unit, students will investigate various facets of the war and discover the effect of the war on American society. Using computer and TV technology greatly enhances the study of history because they allow the teacher to present material in a new and dynamic way. They also provide the student with an opportunity to investigate primary source materials.

Unit Tools

INTERDISCIPLINARY LINK

Language Arts: Students will utilize proper use of grammar in developing multimedia presentations about various aspects of the Civil War. They will create suitable "scripts" and develop concepts regarding topics relating to the conflict.

SPOTLIGHT ON TECHNOLOGY

Internet Research: Students will use the World Wide Web to collect data. They will also use the information that they collect, as well as data from traditional sources, to develop multimedia presentations.

Word Processing: Students will use word processing software to assist them in collecting information from Web resources, making presentations, and providing reports about their findings to the instructor.

Digital Video (Optional): Students will record their presentations for authentic assessment purposes.

TECHNOLOGY RESOURCES NEEDED

Hardware
    computers with Internet access
    video or DVD player
    printer to provide "hard copy" of student work and resources for evaluation

Software
    Web browsing software
    word processing software
    presentation software

SECTION 2—RESOURCE UNITS

WEB, LITERATURE, AND VIDEO RESOURCES

Web Resources

Abraham Lincoln Papers Collection (Library of Congress):
http://memory.loc.gov/ammem/alhtml/malhome.html

American Civil War Homepage: **http://sunsite.utk.edu/civil-war/**

Battle of Fredericksburg Official Records and Battle Description:
www.civilwarhome.com/fredrick.htm

Born in Slavery: Slave Narratives From the Federal Writers Project (1936–1938):
http://memory.loc.gov/ammem/snhtml/snhome.html

Camp Life: Civil War Collections From Gettysburg:
www.cr.nps.gov/museum/exhibits/gettex/

CivilWar@Smithsonian: **http://civilwar.si.edu/**

Civil War Battles by State: **www2.cr.nps.gov/abpp/battles/bystate.htm**

Civil War Preservation Trust: **www.civilwar.org**

eHistory: American Civil War: **www.ehistory.com/uscw/index.cfm**

1862 Peninsula Campaign: **www.peninsulacampaign.org**

Eyewitness to History: The American Civil War:
www.eyewitnesstohistory.com/cwfrm.htm

Hargrett Library Rare Map Collection: The American Civil War:
http://scarlett.libs.uga.edu/darchive/hargrett/maps/civil.html

Historical Natural History: Insects and the Civil War:
http://scarab.msu.montana.edu/historybug/civilwar2/civilwar.htm

Joshua Lawrence Chamberlain and Little Round Top Worksheet:
www.vcsc.k12.in.us/staff/mhutchison/ice2000/chamberlain.htm

Letters From an Iowa Soldier in the Civil War:
www.civilwarletters.com/home.html

Library of Congress: Civil War:
http://memory.loc.gov/ammem/aaohtml/exhibit/aopart4.html

Library of Congress: Civil War Maps Collection:
http://memory.loc.gov/ammem/gmdhtml/cwmhtml/cwmhome.html

The Life of Civil War Private Jefferson Moses: **www.ioWeb.com/civilwar/**

Manassas Battlefield History:
www.nps.gov/mana/battlefield_history/bhistory.htm

Mr. Lincoln's Virtual Library (Library of Congress):
http://memory.loc.gov/ammem/alhtml/alhome.html

"My Precious Loulie...": Love Letters of the Civil War:
http://spec.lib.vt.edu/cwlove/

PBS: Abraham and Mary Lincoln: A House Divided:
www.pbs.org/wgbh/amex/lincolns/

PBS: The Civil War: **www.pbs.org/civilwar/**

PBS: The Civil War Classroom Activities:
www.pbs.org/civilwar/classroom/activities.html

Professor Bernie Dodge's Civil War Page:
http://edWeb.sdsu.edu/people/bdodge/scaffold/CW/warWeb.html

Related Resources for Civil War Projects (teacher-created resource page with resources): **www.vcsc.k12.in.us/staff/mhutchison/civilwar/**

Valley of the Shadow: **http://valley.vcdh.virginia.edu/**

War for States' Rights: **http://civilwar.bluegrass.net/**

Weapons of the Civil War: **http://165.29.91.7/classes/humanities/amstud/97-98/weapons/CIVIL~1.HTM**

THE CIVIL WAR: A MULTIMEDIA INVESTIGATION

Literature Resources

All for the Union: The Civil War Diary and Letters of Elisha Hunt Rhodes, Elisha Hunt Rhodes

The American Heritage New History of the Civil War, Bruce Catton, James M. McPherson, & Noah Andre Trudeau

The Americans (U.S. history textbook), Houghton Mifflin (Publisher)

April 1865, Jay Winnick

Battle Cry of Freedom, James McPherson

"Bayonet! Forward": My Civil War Reminiscences, Joshua Lawrence Chamberlain

The Civil War: A Narrative, Shelby Foote

The Civil War: An Illustrated History, Geoffrey Ward, Ric Burns, & Ken Burns

The Civil War Archive: The History of the Civil War in Documents, Henry Steele Commager

Company Aytch; Or, a Side Show of the Big Show and Other Sketches, Sam Watkins

Introduction to the Social Studies, John J. Bonstingl

Killer Angels, Michael Shaara

Landscape Turned Red, Stephan Sears

The Library of Congress Civil War Desk Reference, Margaret Wagner

The Red Badge of Courage, Stephen Crane

Terrible Swift Sword, Bruce Catton

Video Resources

Abraham and Mary Lincoln: A House Divided (PBS Home Video)

The Civil War (PBS Home Video)

Gettysburg (Warner Home Video)

Unchained Memories: Readings From the Slave Narratives (HBO Home Video)

teaching the unit

DAY 1 Students are introduced to the lesson, and materials are distributed, including permission slips, project requirement sheets, and topic lists. One way the teacher might introduce this lesson and its historical background is to have students view *Unchained Memories: Readings From the Slave Narratives,* a 2003 HBO production that featured readings from the *WPA Slave Narratives,* as collected in the Library of Congress. (If the teacher is using the unit as a lesson on how a historian gathers and interprets evidence, then a discussion of various methods of collecting historical resources might be in order.)

DAY 2 The teacher may wish to continue distribution of materials, as well as remind students to return permission slips. *(Note:* While the materials in *The Civil War, Abraham and Mary Lincoln: A House Divided,* and *Gettysburg* would not be

SECTION 2—RESOURCE UNITS

considered offensive or controversial, necessarily, it is recommended to have parents consent to the project in writing simply for them to understand the nature of the assignment, that it is an "alternative assignment," and to notify students about how to contact the teacher in case a parent has questions or concerns.)

DAY 3 Students should form groups and select topics. Students may select a topic from the topic list provided or may, with teacher approval, select a topic not on the list. Distribute "portfolios" (manila folders) to students so they can keep materials they collect online or in text format. Completed portfolios will make up a portion of the student grades.

DAY 4 Students begin library orientation with the school media specialist, who will show them how to effectively search for materials in library stacks. Students view the first part of the "Little Round Top" segment of the film *Gettysburg*.

DAY 5 Complete the segment of *Gettysburg*. Have students complete the activity worksheet "Joshua Lawrence Chamberlain and Little Round Top" (available at **www.vcsc.k12.in.us/staff/mhutchison/ice2000/chamberlain.htm**).

DAY 6 Students turn in the worksheet "Joshua Lawrence Chamberlain and Little Round Top." Have students work on the Internet scavenger hunt in class. Ask them to turn in the Scavenger Hunt worksheet before the end of the class period.

DAYS 7–10 Students work on creating presentations based on criteria set by the teacher. This includes students using the index feature of *The Civil War* to view information from the series regarding their project topic.

DAY 11 Students submit portfolios for a briefing. The teacher checks to see if the group is successfully collaborating and has completed significant research toward the finished project.

DAYS 12–14 Students construct presentations based on their research.

DAY 15 Student groups demonstrate projects to peers.

TEACHING TIPS The teacher might wish to allot for one or two extra days for student collaborative work, simply to provide a cushion in case of some unexpected obstruction (such as weather delay, school event, network breakdown, etc.).

THE CIVIL WAR: A MULTIMEDIA INVESTIGATION

Also, should the teacher feel that it is necessary to provide more time for collaboration and presentation completion, the video aspect of the unit can be reduced. In addition, the scavenger hunt segment of the lesson can be reduced or eliminated.

Civil War Project
Topics

This list offers topics you might want to consider for your Civil War projects. Some of these project ideas will be well known to you; others you may need to research a little before making your selection. Once you select a topic, you are expected to stay with it for the duration of the assignment. Once a topic is selected, it cannot be selected by any other group in the class. Feel free to see me for more information. I will consider any topic you might want to pursue that is not on this list.

- Underlying causes of the Civil War
- Fort Sumter
- Bull Run (Manassas)
- Joshua Lawrence Chamberlain and Little Round Top
- Role of slavery in the Civil War (abolitionist movement)
- Comparing Abraham Lincoln and Jefferson Davis
- "Billy Yank and Johnny Reb": Ordinary soldiers in the Civil War (Elisha Hunt Rhodes and Sam Watkins)
- Comparing Grant and Lee
- Grant and Lee at Appomattox
- Ironclad ships
- Battle of Antietam
- Comparing Confederate generals (Jackson, Stuart, Longstreet, etc.) with Union generals (McClellan, Burnside, etc.)
- Civil War medicine
- Emancipation Proclamation
- Sullivan Ballou letter (letters of Civil War era soldiers)
- Peninsula Campaign
- Women in the Civil War (Clara Barton, Mary Chestnut, "Mother" Bickerdyke)
- Civil War photography
- Battle of Gettysburg, Day 1
- Battle of Gettysburg, Day 2
- Battle of Gettysburg, Day 3
- Daily life in a town or city of the North compared with a town or city of the South
- Siege of Vicksburg
- Wilderness Campaign
- Andersonville Prison
- Sherman's March
- Lincoln assassination
- Effect of the war on black rights and civil rights
- Battle of Shiloh
- New inventions (warfare) in the Civil War
- Civil War espionage

NETS•S CURRICULUM SERIES: SOCIAL STUDIES UNITS FOR GRADES 9–12

SECTION 2—RESOURCE UNITS

LESSON EXTENDERS Ask students to follow up their multimedia presentation with a "living history" unit, perhaps a role-playing exercise of leaders or primary figures of the Civil War era, such as Abraham Lincoln, U. S. Grant, Robert E. Lee, or "Stonewall" Jackson.

Have students do comparison studies of the Civil War with other conflicts in U.S. history. For example, they could compare two conflicts based on benchmarks such as length of conflict, number of casualties, cost, and other factors.

Have students create original video presentations of their research findings that can be posted online.

Assessment

CRITERIA	1 UNSATISFACTORY	2 SATISFACTORY	3 EXEMPLARY	SCORE
SOCIAL STUDIES STANDARDS				
Understanding of how human beings view themselves in and over time	Understanding is not in evidence.	Student demonstrates acceptable understanding within the context of this project.	Student demonstrates exemplary understanding, making connections to personal experience through higher level applications of thinking.	
Understanding of how people create and change structures of power, authority, and governance	Understanding is not in evidence.	Student demonstrates acceptable understanding within the context of this project.	Student demonstrates exemplary understanding, making connections to personal experience through higher level applications of thinking.	
Recognition of the ideals, principles, and practices of citizenship in a democratic republic	Understanding is not in evidence.	Student demonstrates acceptable understanding within the context of this project.	Student demonstrates exemplary understanding, making connections to personal experience through higher level applications of thinking.	
NETS				
Understanding of social, ethical, and human issues related to technology	Understanding is not in evidence.	Student demonstrates acceptable understanding within the context of this project.	Student demonstrates exemplary understanding, making connections to personal experience through higher level applications of thinking.	
Use of technology productivity tools	Student shows lack of minimum proficiency in using these tools.	Student meets minimum proficiency for using these tools.	Student goes beyond minimum proficiency for using these tools, applying their use beyond the requirements of this project.	
Use of technology research tools	Student shows lack of minimum proficiency in using these tools.	Student meets minimum proficiency for using these tools.	Student goes beyond minimum proficiency for using these tools, applying their use beyond the requirements of this project.	
			Subtotal Points	

continued next page

Assessment

CRITERIA	1 UNSATISFACTORY	2 SATISFACTORY	3 EXEMPLARY	SCORE
PROJECT				
Project design	Project does not include a storyboard or the portfolio is missing evidence of the planning process.	Project includes a storyboard and a portfolio documenting the planning process.	Project includes a storyboard, a portfolio documenting the planning process, and evidence of thorough research.	
Project format	Project is hard to navigate, and has illegible text and/or distracting graphics and special effects.	Project has simple navigation and legible text. Layout graphics do not distract from the presentation of content.	Project has intuitive navigation and legible text. Layout graphics enhance the presentation of content.	
Project creativity	Student uses graphics without attributing sources or lacks a follow-up task that invites the audience to extend their understanding of the content.	Student uses graphics with proper citation of sources and includes at least one activity that invites the audience to complete a content-related task on- or offline.	Student uses original graphics and interactive features that challenge the audience to use the site content meaningfully online.	
Project requirements	The group did not follow directions including elements listed in the guidelines.	The group followed directions including most elements listed in the guidelines.	The group followed directions including all elements listed in the guidelines.	
Project accuracy	The facts presented include inaccuracies and do not include proper documentation.	The facts presented are accurate and partially documented.	The facts presented are accurate and well documented, with embedded links where appropriate.	
PRESENTATION				
Presentation: speaking	Speaker is difficult to understand. Serious grammatical errors are evident.	Voice is clear. Some minor grammatical errors are evident.	Voice is clear and easy to understand. Correct grammar is used.	
Presentation: use of technology	Student demonstrates lack of mastery of technology, which negatively affects the effectiveness of the presentation.	Student demonstrates proficient use of technology. The use of technology increases the effectiveness of the presentation.	Student demonstrates exemplary use of technology. The use of technology significantly increases the effectiveness of the presentation.	
Presentation: length	Either the presentation does not meet the time requirement as specified in the guidelines or the use of time is not effective.	Presentation meets time requirement as set in the guidelines and includes the effective use of resources.	Presentation meets time requirement set in the guidelines, but also includes quality use of time in regard to information and resources demonstrated.	
Presentation: mastery of content	Student demonstrates a lack of knowledge of the project subject.	Student demonstrates effective mastery of the project subject.	Student demonstrates exemplary mastery of content of the project subject.	
Presentation: response to questions	Student is unable to answer questions regarding the project, or the answers are incomplete.	Student is proficient in answering questions concerning the project.	Student demonstrates confidence in answering questions regarding the project.	
			Total Points	

SECTION 2—RESOURCE UNITS

Additional Resources

The following pages provide samples of materials to use in this project.

RESOURCE PAGE   Create a page on your school's Web site to direct students to additional resources. One example is at **www.vcsc.k12.in.us/staff/mhutchison/civilwar** (Figure 3).

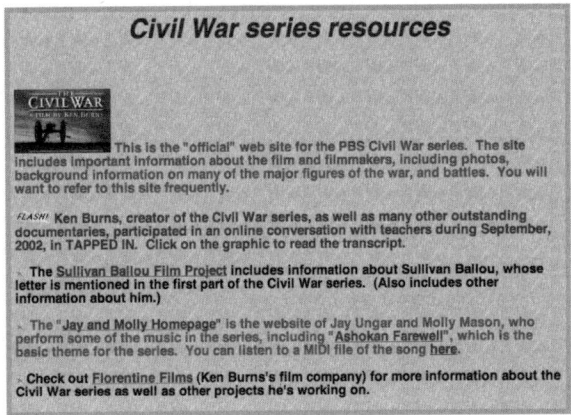

FIGURE 3. Example of a teacher-created resource page.

Civil War Project
Requirements Checklist

Presentation

Make sure your project meets or exceeds the following requirements. Submit this sheet with your portfolio.

_____ 1. The presentation must be at least **three minutes long**. (Be sure to use slide timings. Check with the teacher if you have questions. Use Rehearse Timings in the Slide Show menu of PowerPoint.)

_____ 2. Your **title slide** must have the full names of everyone in your group, the class period, and the subject that you researched. You must also have a picture relating to the subject you researched on the title slide.

_____ 3. You must have at least **four sound files** in the presentation, either from something related to the Civil War or from PowerPoint.

_____ 4. You must have at least **five pictures** in the presentation. These can be from something related to the Civil War series or relating to the particular subject area you researched.

_____ 5. One slide must have a **summary** of the subject you researched that states the significance of that topic.

_____ 6. Your last slide should be a **bibliography** citing all works used. You must use *The Civil War* series and at least four other sources. Each bibliography entry must include the author, title, page number, year of publication, publisher name, and place of publication. Any Web source must include the URL (Web address).

_____ 7. Make sure you have followed all the other requirements mentioned in the other handouts you have received.

continued next page

Civil War Project Requirements Checklist—page 2

Portfolio

Make sure your portfolio (your manila folder) meets or exceeds the following requirements. Submit this sheet with your portfolio.

Your portfolio should include:

_____ 1. All storyboards used to develop the presentation.

_____ 2. Hard copies (either printed or photocopied) of all research done on this project.

_____ 3. Copies of all rough drafts, notes, and other text related to the project.

_____ 4. Thumbnails of each slide used in the presentation. (When you are ready to do this, go to the File menu in PowerPoint, select Print, and click the Handouts view in Print What.)

All projects are due no later than the end of the period on **March 21**. You are welcome to submit your project earlier if you'd like a preliminary evaluation. (I'll look at it and give you pointers on how to increase your score.)

Evaluation Notes to Consider

1. The finished product includes a completed portfolio and completed PowerPoint presentation, stored in a network folder.
2. The maximum value of the assignment is 75 points.
3. Portfolios will be collected and evaluated prior to the project due date.
4. Each student in the group will be awarded the same grade.
5. Each group will be graded according to criteria established in the grading rubric to be provided. Criteria will include the completion of the portfolio, creativity, the length of the presentation, adherence to presentation requirements, and the group presentation (see the rubric for more details).
6. The deadline for the project has been set. Presentations are due on that date or before without exception. Groups may submit a presentation prior to the due date for a preliminary evaluation. The group may elect to accept the preliminary grade as their final grade or to make the suggested changes to increase their total score.
7. Project grades will be figured in the second six weeks of the grading period.
8. Each group will store their presentation during construction and after completion in a computer network folder. The teacher will demonstrate how to do this.
9. All presentations will be "burned" to CD and will eventually be available for download from a Web page on the school Web server.
10. Students should be aware that some presentation work may need to be completed outside of class time.
11. The teacher will issue passes to students or groups to use computers in the Media Center at times other than class time. Any student deemed disruptive by the teacher or the media specialist while working on this project will receive a grade reduction.
12. These criteria will be updated as the project progresses. Look for updates.

Civil War Project

Scavenger Hunt

Looking online, answer all the following questions before the end of the period today. *(Hints:* You will probably want to use a search engine such as Google at **www.google.com** to find answers. Also, remember there is a Web page designed specifically for the Civil War project at **www.vcsc.k12.in.us/ staff/mhutchison/civilwar.)**

1. As of today, what are the standings (team names, locations, and win/loss records) of all the teams in the National Basketball Association Central Division?

2. Find the name, political party, and current street address of the attorney general of Illinois.

3. Find at least two e-mail lists that are moderated or hosted by your teacher. Name these two lists, as well as the Web addresses where one can look at past posts.

4. What was the number two watched TV show during the past week, according to the Nielsen Ratings? Also, provide the rating, share, and number of households watching this show.

5. Describe any two pictures you see at the top of the page of the Classroom Connect Web site.

6. What is the date that the 2005 Indianapolis 500 is scheduled to be run? Since the first race, how many 500s have been run? Who won the 2004 Indianapolis 500? Also, write the Web address for the Indianapolis 500 Web site.

7. Find the Web address for the Abraham Lincoln Presidential Library and Museum. Write the address below. Also, write the Lincoln quote you find on the home page.

8. What year was Ken Burns born? From which college did he graduate? Write the Web address where you found this information.

9. Write the names of any three minor league teams that feed into the St. Louis Cardinals major league baseball team. Provide the name of the team the Cardinals will face on opening day of the 2005 baseball season. Will this be a home game or an away game?

10. Who is David Kenyon Webster? What did he do? How did he die? Write the Web address of the site created in his honor.

11. Name Ken Burns' film company. Name two films he has made for PBS (other than The Civil War).

12. What album won Album of the Year honors at this year's Grammy Awards? Write the Web address where you found this information.

13. Write the place where the 2005 Academy Awards ceremony will be held. What is the scheduled date for the awards ceremony?

14. Write your birth date below. Tell me the motion picture that was named Best Picture for the year you were born. Who were the producers of that year's Best Picture?

15. Where do the Indianapolis Colts hold their preseason training camp? Write the Web address where you found that information.

Civil War Project
Evaluation Rubric

Group Members:

Project Subject:

Class Period:

Evaluation Criteria

1. Portfolio Completion
   (The portfolio should include storyboards and a hard copy of the resources used.)
   15 points total

   _____ points awarded

2. Presentation Length
   (Did the presentation last at least three minutes?)
   10 points total

   _____ points awarded

3. Creativity
   (What did the group do to develop a unique project? This includes the creative use of pictures, sound clips, and other forms of media.)
   20 points total

   _____ points awarded

4. Presentation Requirements
   (Requirements include the proper creation of a title slide, the use of at least four sources besides the *Civil War* series, and the other elements indicated in the project requirement sheet.)
   20 points total

   _____ points awarded

5. Group Presentation
   (How did the group present their project to the class?)
   10 points total

   _____ points awarded

Final Evaluation Score (Addition of 1–5 above.)
   75 points total

   Group Points Grade: _____

   Group Letter Grade: _____

Instructor Comments: _____

_____

America's representational government, founded on capital.

Money, Special Interest Groups, and Reelection Rates

MATHEW MANWELLER

"Winning isn't everything; it's the only thing."

Vince Lombardi

UNIT OBJECTIVES

Students will be challenged to:

- Research the role of money in federal congressional elections and its effect on them.
- Identify variables, other than money, that affect U.S. reelection rates.
- Compare and contrast the election strategies of incumbents and challengers.
- Investigate, with content area experts, why some candidates win despite being outspent.
- Use software and the Internet to collect, analyze, and report data.
- Develop causal hypotheses.

SOCIAL STUDIES STANDARDS ADDRESSED

V **Individuals, Groups, and Institutions**
Social studies programs should include experiences that provide for the study of interactions among individuals, groups, and institutions.

VI **Power, Authority, and Governance**
Social studies programs should include experiences that provide for the study of how people create and change structures of power, authority, and governance.

X **Civic Ideals and Practices**
Social studies programs should include experiences that provide for the study of the ideals, principles, and practices of citizenship in a democratic republic.

NETS•S ADDRESSED

3 **Technology Productivity Tools**
- Students use technology tools to enhance learning, increase productivity, and promote creativity.
- Students use productivity tools to collaborate in constructing technology-enhanced models, preparing publications, and producing other creative works.

4 **Technology Communications Tools**
- Students use telecommunications to collaborate, publish, and interact with peers, experts, and other audiences.
- Students use a variety of media and formats to communicate information and ideas effectively to multiple audiences.

5 **Technology Research Tools**
- Students use technology to locate, evaluate, and collect information from a variety of sources.
- Students use technology tools to process data and report results.
- Students evaluate and select new information resources and technological innovations based on the appropriateness to specific tasks.

6 **Technology Problem-Solving and Decision-Making Tools**
- Students use technology resources for solving problems and making informed decisions.
- Students employ technology in the development of strategies for solving problems in the real world.

MONEY, SPECIAL INTEREST GROUPS, AND REELECTION RATES

CENTRAL DISCIPLINE AREA

Campaign Finance

The confluence of democracy and capitalism often raises the issues of fair elections, the role of money in campaigns, and the power of incumbency. In recent years, campaign finance reform has been a powerful political movement in the United States, at the national as well as the state level. In this unit, students will be challenged to investigate the role of money in U.S. elections and draw conclusions about the effect that money has on reelection rates. In an era of increasing student cynicism, it is important to ask the question, "Can money really buy an election?"

UNIT DESCRIPTION

This unit launches the entire class into a collective research project about the role of money in U.S. elections. Working in small groups, individually, and as an entire class, students will investigate current congressional reelection rates and the typical amounts of money raised by incumbents and challengers, as well as identify cases in which the candidate raising and spending the most money does not win. After identifying winners who have spent less, students will form research groups to examine online newspapers and participate in asynchronous telecommunications with area experts. Their goal will be to explain why some candidates win despite being outspent. The unit will conclude with written reports and class presentations summarizing the research findings.

Unit Tools

INTERDISCIPLINARY LINKS

Language Arts: Students will draft a final report summarizing their research findings. They will develop hypotheses and construct organized and clearly articulated written arguments about the role of money in elections. The paper will include statistical data, interview dialogue, and information from online newspapers.

Mathematics: Students will collect Federal Election Commission (FEC) data on campaign spending. They will organize financial data in spreadsheets, compute averages and totals, and interpret the data for the purposes of developing hypotheses.

SPOTLIGHT ON TECHNOLOGY

Internet Research: Students will use the Web to collect data on reelection rates, campaign spending, and campaign strategies.

E-Mail Communication: Students will communicate by e-mail with campaign staff, journalists, and political science professors to gain information about campaign strategies.

Spreadsheets: Students will use a spreadsheet to format, analyze, and chart data pertaining to specific past elections.

Word Processing: Students will use word processing software to create a report that summarizes all their findings.

SECTION 2—RESOURCE UNITS

TECHNOLOGY RESOURCES NEEDED

Hardware
computers with Internet and e-mail access
video projector attached to a computer for presentation purposes (optional)
videoconferencing capabilities (optional)

Software
Web browsing software
e-mail program
word processing software
spreadsheet software
presentation software (optional)

WEB AND LITERATURE RESOURCES

Web Resources
2000 Election Statistics:
    http://clerk.house.gov/members/electionInfo/2000/2000Stat.htm
The Big Picture: Election Statistics at a Glance:
    www.opensecrets.org/pubs/bigpicture2000/overview/stats.ihtml
The Brennan Center:
    www.brennancenter.org/programs/programs_dem_cfr.html
The Brookings Institute: Campaign Finance Reform:
    www.brook.edu/gs/cf/cf_hp.htm
Buckley v. Valeo: **http://supct.law.cornell.edu/supct/cases/424us1.htm**
Cast Your Vote: **www.learner.org/exhibits/statistics/**
CATO Handbook for Congress: **www.cato.org/pubs/handbook/hb108/hb108-10.pdf**
Congressional Research Service: **www.contingencies.org/sepoct02/table1.pdf**
Federal Election Commission: **www.fec.gov/finance_reports.html**
How to Lose a House Seat: **www.hillnews.com/news/061703/seat.aspx**
Office of the Clerk, U.S. House of Representatives: Election Information:
    http://clerk.house.gov/members/electionInfo/index.html
Office of the Clerk, U.S. House of Representatives: Election Statistics:
    http://clerk.house.gov/members/electionInfo/elections.html
Political Archive: 1948 Election: **www.rci.rutgers.edu/~eagleton/e-gov/e-politicalarchive-1948election.htm**
Polling Report: **www.pollingreport.com**
Reelection Data, 1790–2000: **www.contingencies.org/sepoct02/table1.pdf**
Reelection Rates Data: **www.opensecrets.org/1994os/osdata/osp6.pdf**
The :30 Second Candidate: **www.pbs.org/30secondcandidate/**
The Usual Suspects: **www.sfusualsuspects.com/history.htm**
Virginia Elections and State Elected Officials Database Project, 1776–2004:
    http://fisher.lib.virginia.edu/collections/stats/valeg/

Literature Resources
Buckley Stops Here: Loosening the Judicial Stranglehold on Campaign Finance Reform, E. Joshua Rosenkranz
Campaign Finance Reform, Anthony Corrado
Financing the 2000 Election, David B. Magleby (Ed.)
Inside Campaign Finance: Myths and Realities, Frank J. Sorauf

MONEY, SPECIAL INTEREST GROUPS, AND REELECTION RATES

Inside the Campaign Finance Battle, Anthony Corrado, Thomas E. Mann, & Trevor Potte (Eds.)

Inside the Campaign Finance Debate: Arguments From the Court Battle Over BCRA, Anthony Corrado (Ed.)

Money and Politics: Financing Our Elections Democratically (The New Democracy Forum), David Donnelly, Janice Fine, Ellen Miller, Joshua Cohen, & Joel Rogers

Money Chase: Congressional Campaign Finance Reform, David B. Magleby & Candice J. Nelson

New Campaign Finance Sourcebook, Anthony Corrado, Thomas Mann, Daniel Ortiz, & Trevor Potter

Political Money: Deregulating American Politics, Selected Writings on Campaign Finance Reform, Annelise Anderson (Ed.)

Unfree Speech: The Folly of Campaign Finance Reform, Bradley A. Smith

User's Guide to Campaign Finance Reform, Gerald C. Lubenow (Ed.)

Voting With Dollars: A New Paradigm for Campaign Finance, Ian Ayres & Bruce A. Ackerman

DAY 1

In some fashion, students should be introduced to reelection rates for members of Congress (House and Senate). One option is for the teacher to lecture on this topic. The other option is to create a WebQuest on the topic. A variety of Web resources highlighting reelection rates have been provided in the Web Resources section of this unit. It is important that students understand that incumbents rarely lose elections.

If creating a WebQuest is too time consuming, the following alternative will work. Have students visit **www.contingencies.org/sepoct02/table1.pdf,** or project the Web site for the whole class using a projection device. The Web site highlights retention rates for Congress for the past 200 years. Students will see that for the past few decades, turnover rates have hovered around 10%, much lower than the historical average. Have students brainstorm the advantages and disadvantages of having little turnover in Congress. You may want to create two lists on the board. Or, you may want to hold an impromptu debate. Regardless, students should be led to consider the following points: too little turnover results in uncompetitive elections, members of Congress being unresponsive to constituents, and few new people or ideas brought to Congress. However, in response, too much turnover can eliminate experienced representatives and experts in specific types of legislation, and sometimes, small states can gain power in Congress only if they have a long-serving member who has risen to a leading position on a powerful committee. As the instructor, you may want to ask the class to decide whether the benefits of higher turnover rates outweigh the costs.

In addition, teachers may want to introduce students to important tangential issues related to campaign financing, such as:

- FEC rules about campaign donation limits
- *Buckley v. Valeo* (campaign donations as free speech)
- Gerrymandering

DAY 2 Students need to collect information about which candidates won and lost in the 2000 elections. (The 2000 election should be used because the FEC requires time to compile important financial data and summarize it in a manner high school students can understand. The FEC may not have summarized data for more recent elections.) Students should be placed in cooperative learning groups for this stage of the project. Each group should be assigned one state to study. Each group will access the Office of the Clerk's Election Statistics site at **http://clerk.house.gov/members/electionInfo/elections.html**. At the site, student groups will be able to find data illustrating who won and lost every House and Senate race for a particular year (including vote totals). Students should select the year 2000, find their state, and transfer the data to a spreadsheet they will use later.

DAY 3 Students need to access the Federal Election Commission Web site at **www.fec.gov/finance_reports.html**. Following the links to the 2000 state elections, students can determine which candidate was the incumbent or challenger, and who received and spent the most money. Students should record the data in their spreadsheet next to the data they recorded the previous day. The spreadsheet should contain the following information:

- State and district number
- House or Senate race
- Which candidate won
- Which candidate was the incumbent
- How much each candidate spent

Figure 4 illustrates such a spreadsheet. Note that in one case the candidate who spent the most money did not win (Lazio).

FIGURE 4. Students use a spreadsheet to organize statistics from one state's 2000 House and Senate elections.

	A	B	C	D
2	NY Senate Race	Winner	Incumbent	Money Collected
3	Rick Lazio		Open Seat	$38 million
4	Hillary Clinton	X	Open Seat	$29 million
5				
6	NY 14th House District			
7	Carolyn Maloney	X	X	$987,000
8	Carla Rhodes			$29,000
9				
10				

After students have compiled their data, they need to send a copy of the spreadsheet file to the teacher. The teacher needs to compile all the data into one spreadsheet or find a student with good technology skills to accomplish this task (as an extra credit opportunity). Once the data have been compiled, a copy of the compiled data should be sent back to each student (or to one person per group).

DAY 4 Working in groups or individually, students open the spreadsheet they received and begin to identify the elections in which the incumbent lost and elections in which the candidate spending the least money won. (This can be done on a hard copy using a highlighter or electronically by simply using the "Bold" function in the spreadsheet.) Students should create a second spreadsheet with only these congressional races recorded. At the end of the day, the teacher should bring the class together to ensure that everyone has identified the same congressional races. Some groups may need to edit their spreadsheet data at this point. If they have mistakenly included cases in which the incumbent or the high-spending candidate won, that data should be removed. Or, if they have omitted certain cases, those should be added. The whole class process of examining the data should ensure that everyone has the same data at the end of Day 4.

DAYS 5–7 Each student group needs to be assigned one or two elections that meet the stated criteria. Their task will be to research why the winning candidate won. In essence, they are trying to determine why an "exception" has occurred (incumbent lost or low spender won). The following are way this research can take place:

- Search online newspapers. The *New York Times*, CNN, and ABC News all have Web sites that allow users to search for certain topics. By searching with keywords such as the candidate's name, state, and "senate race," students will have lots of articles to read. *Hint:* If multiple search results are generated, instruct students to examine the articles that were printed just after the election (early November). These tend to be "analysis" articles explaining why a candidate won or lost.
- E-mail members of the campaign staff. All elected officials have Web sites at which constituents can e-mail questions and comments. Students can ask to "speak" with a member of the staff who was involved with the election. Often they are happy to offer their analysis of why their candidate won.
- E-mail political science professors at universities in the state where the election took place. Almost every university has a political science department, and there is almost always at least one professor knowledgeable about local politics. If students e-mail them questions about election strategies many will take the time to reply.
- E-mail journalists at newspapers in the state where the election took place. Journalists tend to be busier than professors, but some will take the time to reply.
- Use "ask an expert" Web sites to investigate why an election resulted as it did.
- For schools and teachers with distance learning facilities, set up a videoconferencing session with any of the people noted above.

SECTION 2—RESOURCE UNITS

DAYS 8–9   Student groups present their findings to the class. After researching why an incumbent lost or why a low spender won, students need to report to the class their hypothesis about why such an event occurred. Depending on their level of technology skills and the amount of time the teacher wants to dedicate to the project, these presentations can take a variety of forms. Simple oral reports will suffice. However, PowerPoint presentations, with spending data, newspaper files, interview transcripts, and e-mail conversations, may be more effective, especially if your students tend to be visual learners. Links included in a PowerPoint presentation can bring the audience directly to primary sources of information online.

DAYS 10–11   Having heard each group's presentation, students need to look for commonalities. First through class discussion and then using a word processor, they should compose a report attempting to answer the following questions:

1. Why do incumbents occasionally lose reelection attempts?

2. Why do candidates who spend less money sometimes win?

Once the class comes to a consensus on answers to these questions, students should attempt to craft a general rule on finance in reelection campaigns. Students should be encouraged to use the research data they collected throughout the unit.

TEACHING TIPS   Take some time to browse the Federal Election Commission and Office of the Clerk Web sites before assigning this project. Both Web sites are intricate and contain lots of information. Your students may become lost. As the teacher, you should be able to direct them to the relevant links within the sites. Putting together an annotated "hotlist" of specific useful pages can be a real time-saver.

Also, when assigning states, make sure that each group receives information on elections in which incumbents lost and low spenders won. Otherwise, students will not be able to complete the second half of the unit. For example, Missouri, New York, and Washington all have 2000 Senate races in which an incumbent lost or the lowest spender won.

LESSON EXTENDERS   Have students write a second report outlining possible reforms to the campaign finance system.

Invite your local state representative to speak to your class, focusing on how raising money affects his or her life as a public servant.

Study candidates in an upcoming election and identify races in which incumbents may most likely lose or in which low spenders have a good chance to win. Students may draw different conclusions as to why incumbents lose or why low spenders win. Students with opposing views could conduct a debate in front of the class.

Create a class Web site that showcases the data that have been analyzed and the conclusions that have been drawn from this project.

Assessment

CRITERIA	1 UNSATISFACTORY	2 SATISFACTORY	3 EXEMPLARY	SCORE
SOCIAL STUDIES STANDARDS				
Understanding of interactions among individuals, groups, and institutions	Understanding is not in evidence.	Student demonstrates acceptable understanding within the context of this project.	Student demonstrates exemplary understanding, making connections to personal experience through higher level applications of thinking.	
Recognition of how people create and change structures of power, authority, and governance	Understanding is not in evidence.	Student demonstrates acceptable understanding within the context of this project.	Student demonstrates exemplary understanding, making connections to personal experience through higher level applications of thinking.	
Understanding of the ideals, principles, and practices of citizenship in a democratic republic	Understanding is not in evidence.	Student demonstrates acceptable understanding within the context of this project.	Student demonstrates exemplary understanding, making connections to personal experience through higher level applications of thinking.	
NETS				
Use of technology productivity tools	Student shows lack of minimum proficiency in using these tools.	Student meets minimum proficiency for using these tools.	Student goes beyond minimum proficiency for using these tools, applying their use beyond the requirements of this project.	
Use of technology communications tools	Student shows lack of minimum proficiency in using these tools.	Student meets minimum proficiency for using these tools.	Student goes beyond minimum proficiency for using these tools, applying their use beyond the requirements of this project.	
Use of technology research tools	Student shows lack of minimum proficiency in using these tools.	Student meets minimum proficiency for using these tools.	Student goes beyond minimum proficiency for using these tools, applying their use beyond the requirements of this project.	
Use of technology problem-solving and decision-making tools	Student shows lack of minimum proficiency in using these tools.	Student meets minimum proficiency for using these tools.	Student goes beyond minimum proficiency for using these tools, applying their use beyond the requirements of this project.	
OTHER CLASS WORK				
Research content and quality	Data set (see Day 3) is incomplete and has many inaccuracies.	Data set is complete, but there are some inaccuracies, or there are no inaccuracies, but data set is incomplete.	Data set is complete and accurate.	
Collaboration and participation	Student completed only one of the research tasks from Days 5–7. Oral report is unorganized and lacking research support.	Student completed two or three of the research tasks from Days 5–7. Oral report utilizes limited research.	Student completed all the research tasks from Days 5–7, and the research is integrated into a well-organized and presented oral report.	
Quality of student work	Written report lacks a clear hypothesis and organizational clarity. Report has numerous grammatical errors.	Written report has a thesis, but it is weakly supported. Report has a moderate number of grammatical errors.	Written report has a clear thesis, and it is well supported and organized. Report has few grammatical errors.	
			Total Points	

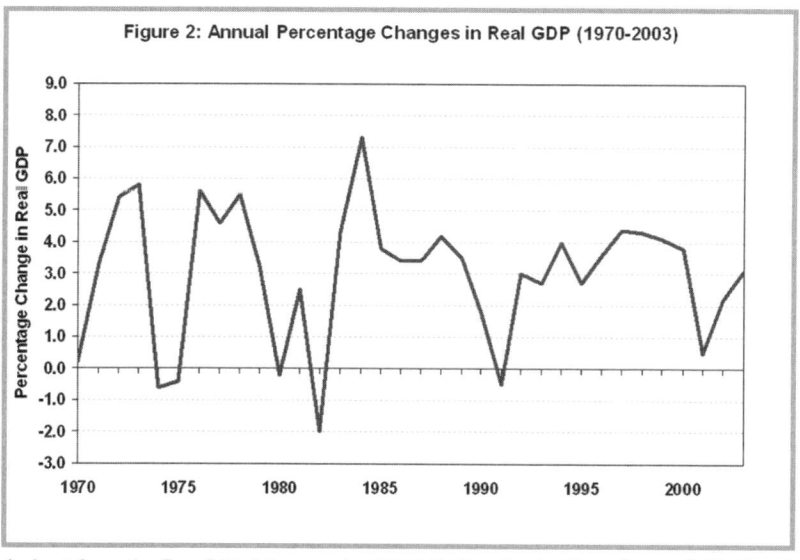

A chart from the EconEdLink lesson plan titled "A Case Study: Gross Domestic Product."

Gross Domestic Product and World Events

DONNA ARCHIBALD

"Prosperity knits a man to the world. He thinks he's 'finding his place in it,' while really it is finding its place in him."

C. S. Lewis

UNIT OBJECTIVES

Student will be challenged to:

- Examine the factors that may determine the U.S. gross domestic product, or GDP.
- Identify the components that make up the gross domestic product.
- Analyze the national and world events that influence the gross domestic product.

SOCIAL STUDIES STANDARDS ADDRESSED

VII **Production, Distribution, and Consumption**
Social studies programs should include experiences that provide for the study of how people organize for the production, distribution, and consumption of goods and services.

NETS•S ADDRESSED

2 **Social, Ethical, and Human Issues**
- Students understand the ethical, cultural, and societal issues related to technology.
- Students practice responsible use of technology systems, information, and software.

3 **Technology Productivity Tools**
- Students use technology tools to enhance learning, increase productivity, and promote creativity.
- Students use productivity tools to collaborate in constructing technology-enhanced models, preparing publications, and producing other creative works.

4 **Technology Communications Tools**
- Students use a variety of media and formats to communicate information and ideas effectively to multiple audiences.

5 **Technology Research Tools**
- Students use technology to locate, evaluate, and collect information from a variety of sources.
- Students use technology tools to process data and report results.

CENTRAL DISCIPLINE AREA

Macroeconomics

Macroeconomics considers the performance of the economy as a whole. Many macroeconomic issues appear in the media on a daily basis. When we study macroeconomics we are looking at topics such as economic growth, inflation, changes in employment, trade, and the success of government policies in keeping our economy strong. This unit focuses on the macroeconomic relationship between our country's gross domestic product and our economy as a whole.

UNIT DESCRIPTION

This unit is intended to be part of instruction about the gross domestic product within an economics course. It is designed as a Web activity that will empower students to research, explore, and find answers about the GDP. It will provide them with an in-depth understanding of the factors that determine the GDP and the way that national and world events affect the various components of the American GDP.

Unit Tools

INTERDISCIPLINARY LINKS

Mathematics: The students will use the equation GDP=C+I+G+X-M to determine the GDP for a specific time frame.

Language Arts: The students will construct a well-developed reflection paper on the material learned.

Speech: The students will participate in an oral presentation on their findings. Forensic speech techniques will be learned.

SPOTLIGHT ON TECHNOLOGY

Internet Research: The students will use the Web for research. Students must seek information on the gross domestic product. They will learn effective searching techniques, the correct evaluation of Internet sites, and the proper format for citing Internet sources.

Spreadsheets: The students will use spreadsheet software to record and analyze data. They will create graphical representations of their findings.

Word Processing: Students will use word processing software tools such as grammar checkers, spelling checkers, margin adjusters, numbering and bullet features, and font formatting utilities to create a report that summarizes their findings.

Desktop Publishing: The students may want use a tool such as PageMaker or AppleWorks to create a print visual to enhance their oral presentation. In the creation of their project, they will consider visual literacy concepts such as alignment, contrast, repetition, and placement of graphics.

Utility Tools: Students may choose to use a photo-editing tool such as Photoshop to edit scanned photos for insertion within their presentation.

Multimedia: The students may want to use a multimedia tool such as PowerPoint, iMovie, Pinnacle, or HyperStudio to create a presentation reflecting their learning. In the creation of their project, they will consider visual literacy concepts such as alignment, contrast, repetition, and placement of graphics.

TECHNOLOGY RESOURCES NEEDED

Hardware
- computers with Internet access
- video projector attached to a computer for presentations
- scanner (optional)

Software
- Web browsing software
- word processing software
- spreadsheet software
- PowerPoint or the PowerPoint viewer
- photo editing software (optional)
- presentation software and/or multimedia software, such as PowerPoint, iMovie, Pinnacle, or HyperStudio (optional)

SECTION 2—RESOURCE UNITS

WEB AND LITERATURE RESOURCES

Web Resources

Backflip: **www.backflip.com**

Bureau of Economic Analysis: **www.bea.doc.gov/bea/dn1.htm**

Commanding Heights: The Battle for the World Economy:
   www.pbs.org/wgbh/commandingheights/lo/index.html

Congressional Budget Office: **www.cbo.gov/index.cfm**

EconEdLink, Data Links: **www.econedlink.org/datalinks/index.cfm**

EconEdLink, EconomicsMinute, A Case Study: Gross Domestic Product:
   www.econedlink.org/lessons/index.cfm?lesson=EM225

EconEdWeb Links: **http://ecedWeb.unomaha.edu/K-12/6-12.cfm**

Economic Indicators: **www.economicindicators.gov**

Economic Report of the President: **http://w3.access.gpo.gov/eop/**

Economics and Statistics Information (U.S. Department of Commerce):
   www.esa.doc.gov

Economics for Tomorrow: **http://eft.merit.edu/index.html**

Economics Statistics Briefing Room: **www.whitehouse.gov/fsbr/output.html**

The First Measured Century: Gross Domestic Product:
   www.pbs.org/fmc/book/14business1.htm

FreeLunch.com From Economy.com: **www.economy.com/freelunch**

Gross Domestic Product Deflator Inflation Calculator:
   www.jsc.nasa.gov/bu2/inflateGDP.html

International Gross Domestic Product Information:
   www.eia.doe.gov/emeu/international/other.html

Kentucky Council on Economic Education (Teachers): **www.econ.org**

Macroeconomics: Online Resources for Students:
   www.fgn.unisg.ch/eurmacro/macroeconomics.html

MSN News: **www.msnbc.com/news/**

National Economic Accounts: **www.bea.doc.gov/bea/dn1.htm**

Teaching Macroeconomics: Brad DeLong's Online Resources:
   www.j-bradford-delong.net/macro_online/

That Money Show: Gross Domestic Product:
   www.pbs.org/wnet/moneyshow/mba/040601.html

U.S. Department of Commerce: **www.commerce.gov**

U.S. Department of Labor, Bureau of Labor Statistics: **www.bls.gov**

The Whitehouse: **www.whitehouse.gov/news/**

World Health Organization: Commission on Macroeconomics and Health:
   www.cmhealth.org

World Wide Web Resources in Economics:
   http://netec.wustl.edu/WebEc/WebEc.html

Literature Resources

Almost Everyone's Guide to Economics, Kenneth Galbraith & Nicole Salinger

Basic Economics: A Citizen's Guide to the Economy, Thomas Sowell

Demystifying Economics, Allen Smith

Dollars & Sense, "When Is a Recession Over?", John Miller

Economic Literacy: What Everyone Needs to Know About Money and Markets, Jacob DeRooy

Economics, Campbell McConnell & Bruce Stanley

Economics, Paul A. Samuelson

GROSS DOMESTIC PRODUCT AND WORLD EVENTS

Economics Explained: Everything You Need to Know About How the Economy Works and Where It Is Going, Robert Heilbroner & Lester Thurow

Economics: The Culture of a Controversial Science, Melvin W. Reder

Fortune Encyclopedia of Economics, "Business Cycles," Christina Romer

Global Trends 2005: An Owner's Manual for the Next Decade, Michael J. Mazarr

Guide to Economic Indicators: Making Sense of Economics, The Economist

How the Markets Really Work, Joel Kurtzman

The Making of Modern Economics: The Lives and Ideas of Great Thinkers, Mark Skousen

Naked Economics: Undressing the Dismal Science, Charles Wheelean

The Nature of Economies, Jane Jacobs

New Ideas From Dead Economists: An Introduction to Modern Economic Thought, Todd G. Buchholz

The New New Economy, Tim McEachern & Chris O'Brien

One Market Under God, Thomas Frank

The Penguin Dictionary of Economics, Graham Bannock, R. E. Baxter, & Evan Davis

The Social Studies Teacher's Book of Lists, Ronald L. Partin

A Student's Guide to Economics, Paul Heyne

Teach Yourself Books: Economics, Bennett Burinham, Martin Cave, & David Higham

PREPARATION Create several free accounts on FreeLunch at Economy.com (**www.economy.com/freelunch**). This Web site will be used to view GDP charts. You will need an e-mail account and a password. An e-mail will be sent to you when you create the account for validation. Follow the link in the e-mail.

DAY 1 Review the four sectors that make up the GDP:

1. Household (consumption)
2. Business (investment)
3. Government (government expenditures)
4. Foreign (exports)

Lead a class discussion about how taxes affect the economy, and the correlation between the GDP and income.

Download the PowerPoint presentation from the EconEdLink lesson plan titled "A Case Study: Gross Domestic Product" found at **www.econedlink.org/lessons/index.cfm?lesson=EM225**. (The presentation will load on your desktop for easy access when you click on the link under "Attention Teachers." This is a free presentation for use in education.)

1. Run the presentation. The second slide contains a graph depicting quarterly changes in real GDP at annual rates from 1990 to 2003. Lead a discussion on trends. Possible questions are:
   - What two years did the United States show negative GDP growth?
   - What do you think happened those two years that may have affected the growth of the GDP?

2. Go to the third slide of the presentation. Lead a discussion comparing the graphs on slide 2 and slide 3. A possible question is:
   - Looking at the years between 1970 and 1980, what growth patterns emerge?

DAYS 2–4 Place the students in pairs. Direct each pair to go to **www.economy.com/freelunch** and log in, then have them complete questions 1–6 in Web Activity One.

Using the information gathered from questions 1–6, instruct the student pairs to create a graph using a spreadsheet program that illustrates their findings. The students should first place the data in the spreadsheet, as in Figure 5.

FIGURE 5. After completing Web Activity One, students input findings into a spreadsheet.

	A	B	C
1	**Item**	Lowest Chained Amount	Highest Chained Amount
2	Gross domestic product	9450	9650
3	Personal consumption expenditures	6590	6750
4	Gross private investment	1588	1633
5	Government consumption	1710	1800
6	Export goods	740	780
7			

Use the data to create a bar graph that presents the information in a graphical form, as in Figure 6.

FIGURE 6. Students convert the spreadsheet data to a chart.

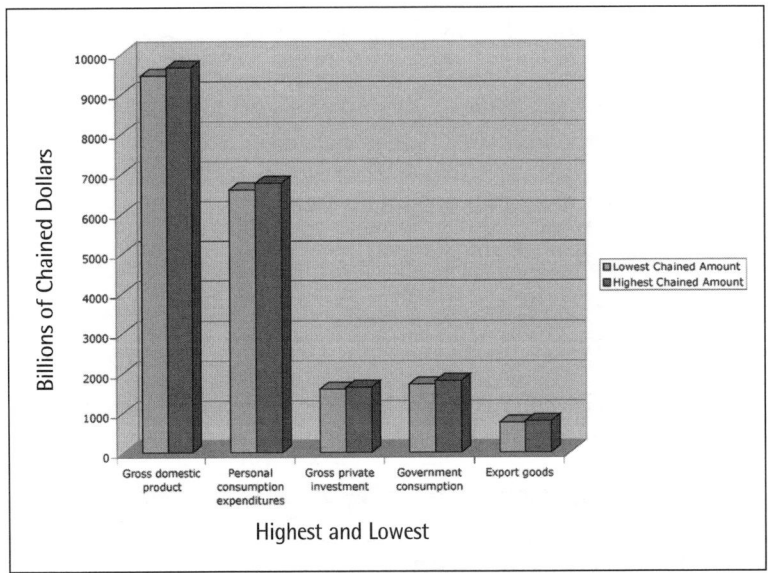

GROSS DOMESTIC PRODUCT AND WORLD EVENTS

Web Activity One

Directions: Go to www.economy.com/freelunch and log in. Click on GDP under the larger heading GDP.

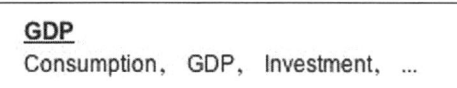

Examine various tables that reflect the current year's gross domestic product by clicking on Table in the Options column.

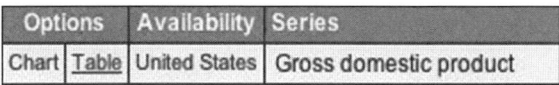

The table will be displayed in a pop-up window. Select Monthly for frequency and Level for transformation. Click Refresh data next to options. Scroll down to view the current year data. To download the table, click United States under Availablility.

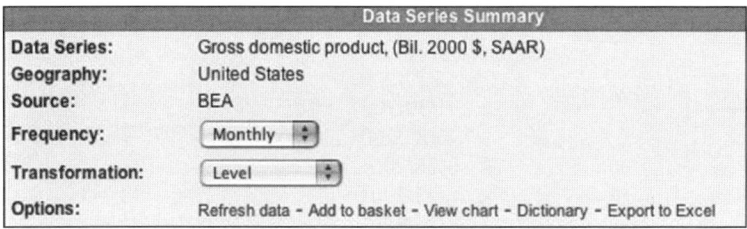

1. Select the Table under Options for the Gross Domestic Product series and answer the following questions:

    When was the lowest chained dollar amount for the year? What was the amount?

    When was the highest chained dollar amount for the year? What was the amount?

2. Select the Table under Options for the Personal Consumption Expenditures series and answer the following questions:

    When was the lowest chained dollar amount for the year? What was the amount?

    When was the highest chained dollar amount for the year? What was the amount?

3. Select the Table under Options for the Gross Private Investment series and answer the following questions:

    When was the lowest chained dollar amount for the year? What was the amount?

    When was the highest chained dollar amount for the year? What was the amount?

4. Select the Table under Options for the Export of Goods series and answer the following questions:

    When was the lowest chained dollar amount for the year? What was the amount?

    When was the highest chained dollar amount for the year? What was the amount?

5. Select the Table under Options for the Government Consumption Expenditures and Gross Investment series and answer the following questions:

    When was the lowest chained dollar amount for the year? What was the amount?

    When was the highest chained dollar amount for the year? What was the amount?

6. Compare and contrast the four tables in steps 2–5. Are there any similaries or patterns? Any notable variances?

7. Using the information from this site and the formula GDP= C+I+G+X-M compute an estimated GDP for a month and year of your choice. Indicate the year and month and show your work.

DAY 5   Lead a discussion about the Web activity that was completed on the previous day. Possible discussion questions include:

- In what area was the smallest growth? How do you think it affected the GDP? By how much?
- Did the personal consumption expenditures show a relevance to seasonal events, such as Christmas?
- How do you think the gross private investment amount correlates with stock transactions?

Check each pair's data sheet and graph for accuracy.

DAYS 6–10   Explain the project to the students as follows:

Each pair will be assigned a case study about the gross domestic product for the following dates.

8/28/2003	3/28/2002
7/31/2003	2/28/2002
6/26/2003	1/31/2002
1/30/2003	12/21/2001
11/26/2002	11/30/2001
10/31/2002	10/31/2001
9/27/2002	9/28/2001
5/24/2002	8/29/2001
4/26/2002	5/25/2001

They will go to the EconEdLink Web page at **www.econedlink.org/lessons/ index.cfm?lesson=EM225** and scroll down to the bottom to find a link to their particular case study. They are to read the first paragraph and not the key economic indicators in the box located at the top of the page. The students will then complete Web Activity Two. After completing Web Activity Two, they will synthesize their learning to create a presentation that provides:

- The GDP in chained dollars.
- An analysis of the two months preceding and the two months after their assigned date. What was the percentage of growth/decline before and after the assigned date?
- An analysis of the chained dollars for household consumption, business investment, government expenditures, and foreign exports. The analysis should include national and world events that may have contributed to the final amount.
- An analysis of goods imported. What effect did they have on the GDP?
- A graphical representation of each component of the GDP.
- A discussion of the effect of imports on GDP.

Web Activity Two

1. Go to www.economy.com/freelunch/ and log on. As in Web Activity One, find the GDP and the components that make up the GDP: personal consumption expenditures, gross private investment, export of goods, and government consumption expenditures and gross investment. Find the chained dollar amount for your assigned time frame and record below.

SERIES	CHAINED DOLLAR
Personal consumption expenditures	
Gross private investment	
Export of goods	
Government consumption expenditures and gross investment	

2. Of the four components, which one is higher? Why do you think it is?

3. On this Web site, they break down the components of personal consumption expenditures. Choose five from the list and examine the charts for these five. List the five below and provide the real chained dollar amount for your time frame.

PERSONAL EXPENDITURE SERIES CHOSEN	REAL CHAINED DOLLARS

4. Using the following Web sites as a beginning, explore the historical events that were taking place during your assigned time frame that may have affected personal expenditures. Using a word processor, analyze the information you find and explain how historical events made people spend more or less during your time frame. The response should be two typed pages. Reference your sources within your explanation. Make sure you provide proper documentation at the end of this Web activity.

   MSN News: www.msnbc.com/news/
   The Whitehouse: www.whitehouse.gov/news/

SECTION 2—RESOURCE UNITS

DAYS 11–12 — Student pairs will give an oral presentation on their findings. They may choose to use multimedia software to create this presentation or to use print visuals to enhance their oral presentation. The teacher will use the oral presentation rubric to assess the presentations.

TEACHING TIPS — Before starting the unit, download the PowerPoint presentation located at EconEdLink, EconomicsMinute, A Case Study: Gross Domestic Product (**www.econedlink.org/lessons/index.cfm?lesson=EM225&page=teacher**). Preview the presentation and make changes as needed.

Provide a list of vocabulary words to each student before the unit begins. As they complete the unit, instruct the students to create their own definition for the words based on their learning.

Organize Internet resources for easy student access:

- File bookmarks on your class browser before starting the unit.
- Use a Web-based bookmark organizer such as Backflip at **www.backflip.com**.
- Create a word processing document with the selected Internet sites and distribute it to students.
- Create a hotlist of resources that your school Webmaster can post on your class Web site for easy access from any location.

LESSON EXTENDERS — Combine the pairs into larger groups to examine a larger time frame. The larger groups will compare data and research to examine trends.

Examine the gross domestic product of a foreign economy and compare its growth with that of the United States.

Have students continue their research using the Web sites in previous exercises and the ones they have found to explore historical events that may have influenced the GDP during their assigned period as a whole and the areas of household consumption, business investment, government expenditures, and exports. Have them use this research to create a presentation. They should keep a log of findings in a word processing document.

Using **www.economy.com/freelunch/**, examine what the United States imports and the amounts.

Author's note: A special thank you to Tom Smith, economics teacher at Elk Grove High School, Township High School District 214, for his assistance.

Assessment

CRITERIA	1 UNSATISFACTORY	2 SATISFACTORY	3 EXEMPLARY	SCORE
SOCIAL STUDIES STANDARDS				
Understanding of how people organize for the production, distribution, and consumption of goods and services	Understanding is not in evidence.	Student demonstrates acceptable understanding within the context of this project.	Student demonstrates exemplary understanding, making connections to personal experience through higher level applications of thinking.	
NETS				
Recognition of the social, ethical, and human issues related to technology	Understanding is not in evidence.	Student demonstrates acceptable understanding within the context of this project.	Student demonstrates exemplary understanding, making connections to personal experience through higher level applications of thinking.	
Use of technology productivity tools	Student shows lack of minimum proficiency in using these tools.	Student meets minimum proficiency for using these tools.	Student goes beyond minimum proficiency for using these tools, applying their use beyond the requirements of this project.	
Use of technology communications tools	Student shows lack of minimum proficiency in using these tools.	Student meets minimum proficiency for using these tools.	Student goes beyond minimum proficiency for using these tools, applying their use beyond the requirements of this project.	
Use of technology research tools	Student shows lack of minimum proficiency in using these tools.	Student meets minimum proficiency for using these tools.	Student goes beyond minimum proficiency for using these tools, applying their use beyond the requirements of this project.	
			Subtotal Points	

continued next page

Assessment

CRITERIA	1 UNSATISFACTORY	2 SATISFACTORY	3 EXEMPLARY	SCORE
RESEARCH				
Research: gathering resources	Student lost focus; therefore, information is not accurate and complete.	Student used a variety of resources, made careful selections, and revised the search when prompted.	Student used a variety of resources, made careful selections, and continually revised the search based on information found.	
Research: using print resources	Student used one resource.	Student used a selection of resources that included one from each: • Reference • Book • Journal	Student used a careful selection of resources that included one from each: • Reference • Book • Journal	
Research: using electronic resources	Student did not make careful selections of electronic resources.	Student selected most of the electronic sources based on: • Authorship • Publisher • Bias • Accuracy • Currency	Student selected all electronic source based on: • Authorship • Publisher • Bias • Accuracy • Currency	
Research: documentation	Student did not provide citations.	Student provided correct citations for most of the sources based on American Psychological Association, Modern Language Association, or *Chicago Manual of Style* conventions.	Student provided correct citations for all sources based on American Psychological Association, Modern Language Association, or *Chicago Manual of Style* conventions.	
GRAPH				
Graph data	Data are disorganized. Graph type is inappropriate, and labels are nonexistent.	Graph type fits the data. Data in tables have appropriate labels. Some disorganization is evident.	Graph type fits the data. Data in tables are well organized with appropriate labels.	
Graph labels	More than five labels are missing.	One or two labels are missing.	The following labels are clearly illustrated in the graph: • A key with color labels for the lowest and highest chained amounts • x and y axes • Title • All five required components	
Graph format	Colors are muted and text is unclear.	Graph is relatively attractive. Colors clash or are in the same hue and do not complement each other. Text is clear.	Graph is well designed, using colors that go together or complement each other. Graph is easily read, the text is clear, and it is visually appealing.	
			Total Points	

The modest bungalows and high-rises of an American city.

How Social Are We Anyway?

CYNDY JONES WOODS

"We are actors playing in a theatre of social systems."

Talcott Parsons

UNIT OBJECTIVES
Students will be challenged to:

- Research and articulate the concepts of role, status, and social class, and use them to describe the connections and interactions of individuals, groups, and institutions in society.

- Analyze group and institutional influences on people, events, and elements of culture in historical and contemporary settings.

- Analyze examples of tensions between expressions of individuality and efforts used to promote social conformity by groups and institutions.

- Describe and examine belief systems basic to specific traditions and laws in contemporary and historical movements.

- Explain and apply ideas and modes of inquiry drawn from behavioral science and social theory in the examination of persistent social issues and problems.

- Effectively use technology to research issues.

- Effectively use technology to create a report of culture and institutions in our society.

SOCIAL STUDIES STANDARDS ADDRESSED

I   Culture
Social studies programs should include experiences that provide for the study of culture and cultural diversity.

IV   Individual Development and Identity
Social studies programs should include experiences that provide for the study of individual development and identity.

V   Individuals, Groups, and Institutions
Social studies programs should include experiences that provide for the study of interactions among individuals, groups, and institutions.

NETS•S ADDRESSED

2   Social, Ethical, and Human Issues
- Students understand the ethical, cultural, and societal issues related to technology.
- Students practice responsible use of technology systems, information, and software.
- Students develop positive attitudes toward technology uses that support lifelong learning, collaboration, personal pursuits, and productivity.

5   Technology Research Tools
- Students use technology to locate, evaluate, and collect information from a variety of sources.
- Students use technology tools to process data and report results.
- Students evaluate and select new information resources and technological innovations based on the appropriateness to specific tasks.

6   Technology Problem-Solving and Decision-Making Tools
- Students use technology resources for solving problems and making informed decisions.
- Students employ technology in the development of strategies for solving problems in the real world.

CENTRAL DISCIPLINE AREAS

Culture and Society

Cultures operate as background filters for decision making and thinking processes. How one reacts to stimuli is often spontaneously generated by cultural training and reinforced by societal interactions. Given that no one culture exists, conflicts are inevitable. Students will be challenged to look at historical influences, institutions, and scientific discoveries and to analyze how these have affected cultures and decisions within our world.

UNIT DESCRIPTION

This unit challenges students to view belief systems that co-mingle and operate within any society. These systems create tension and conflict, even while illustrating the need for changes and adaptations in our dynamic world. The students will collaborate and cooperate in identifying major institutions that have and will continue to affect them, the way they view their world, and where they choose to live. As they identify these institutions and institutional beliefs, they will compare and contrast them within their own community. After the initial identification, students will research selected communities and their dominant institutions. Research results will be examined to synthesize trends and their manifestation within the community. Demographic and census information will be researched and analyzed, and compared with anecdotal trends. Results then will be presented to the whole class.

Unit Tools

INTERDISCIPLINARY LINKS

Language Arts: Students will prepare a final summary report, comparing and contrasting the local community cultures with the assigned community cultures. Research data will be included, as well as anecdotal information gathered from online sources.

Mathematics: Within the final summary report, students will determine significant indicators of culture and ascertain the frequency with which they appear within the selected communities. This information will be graphically displayed, as well as interpreted, to provide further information about how belief systems are intertwined. Students will use averages and medians to summarize the information.

SPOTLIGHT ON TECHNOLOGY

Internet Research: Students will use the Internet to gather information on trends, anecdotal evidence, culture presentations, institution guidelines, population data, census data, and historical information.

E-Mail Communication: Students will e-mail students at other communities with questionnaires, and analyze the returned data.

Word Processing: Students will generate reports and graphs using word processing software.

TECHNOLOGY RESOURCES NEEDED

Hardware
    computers with Internet and e-mail access
    printer
    video presentation system (optional)

Software
    word processing program
    spreadsheet program
    presentation or slideshow program (optional)

SECTION 2—RESOURCE UNITS

WEB AND LITERATURE RESOURCES

Web Resources

Arizona Republic: **http://azcentral.com**
Blue Laws: **www.bartleby.com/65/bl/bluelaws.html**
Google: **www.google.com**
Gotham Gazette: NYC's Blue Laws:
   www.gothamgazette.com/article/issueoftheweek/20030526/200/405
Houghton Mifflin Blue Laws: **http://college.hmco.com/history/readerscomp/rcah/html/ah_011100_bluelaws.htm**
New York City Blue Laws:
   www.gothamgazette.com/article/issueoftheweek/20030526/200/405
New York Times Sociology:
   http://college.nytimes.com/guests/directory/Social_Sciences/Sociology/
U.S. Census Bureau: **www.census.gov**
Wikipedia Blue Laws: **http://en.wikipedia.org/wiki/Blue_law**
YellowPages.com: **http://yellowpages.com**

Literature Resources

America Behind the Color Line: Dialogues With African Americans, Henry Louis Gates
Babbitt, Sinclair Lewis
Boys' War: Confederate and Union Soldiers Talk About the War, Jim Murphy
Class: A Guide Through the American Status System, Paul Fussell
Culture of Fear: Why Americans Are Afraid of the Wrong Things, Barry Glassner
The Great Gatsby, F. Scott Fitzgerald
How Class Works: Power and Social Movement, Stanley Aronowitz
Native Son, Richard Wright
Navajos, Ruth Underhill
The Outsiders, S. E. Hinton
Race, Class, and Gender in the United States: An Integrated Study, Paula S. Rothenberg
Roll of Thunder, Hear My Cry, Mildred Taylor
We Talk, You Listen: New Tribes, New Turf, Vine Deloria
Where We Stand: Class Matters, Bell Hooks

teaching the unit

DAY 1 The first day will set the tone for tolerance and will encourage students to hone their observation skills. Begin with a writing exercise. Have the students write five statements about themselves. Tell them to begin each statement with "I am." To avoid leading the students, give a generic example: "I am a human." Typically this will take only about five minutes. Limit the statements to five. Lead a discussion on five statements that you choose to divulge. My five "I am" statements are:

> I am a wife.
>
> I am a mother.
>
> I am an animal lover.
>
> I am a nature lover.
>
> I am curious.

Dissecting each of the statements gives the students a clearer picture of me and what I consider important. The things that are important to me may not be important to them. The main goal of this exercise is to help students understand that each of us comes with individual and personal ideas of what life is and is meant to be. My ideas are no more important than anyone else's, but they're mine. Tolerating ideas that are different from our own promotes harmonious interactions and a rich and varied society.

This will lead to a discussion of why these personal beliefs are important. In my cultural framework, a wife and mother represent the ability to commit and share. Is that what others believe? Slowly tease out what the students think and what they might share as important ideals. Blend this with what they see as important for their world.

Introduce the homework assignment. They will be interviewing two high school students—not in this class—and reporting the findings the following day. The interviewees are to remain anonymous. The important element is the information gathered, which will be compiled on Day 2. Have students ask their two interviewees the questions and carefully record their responses.

DAY 2 In groups of four, have students tally their data from their interviews. Then, tally all the information on the board. Ask students if they see any trends. Are there many of the interviewees with religious backgrounds? Are there many whose grandparents were not born in the U.S.? What is the average number of kids that the interviewees want to have?

Looking at the data will lead to the overall assumptions that can be made about this culture—in this high school. Help students to draw conclusions or to determine that there is not enough information to draw conclusions. What other information would have been useful to gather? Does this information apply to students across town? Why or why not? Would students consider this a snapshot of all high school students in town?

Point out that students are influenced by their background cultures. How many of the "I am" statements included references to gender, race, or religion? Are some questions more personal than others?

What data are collected by the U.S. Census? How can data collection be helpful?

Day 1 Homework Assignment

QUESTION	INTERVIEWEE ONE	INTERVIEWEE TWO
What is your age?		
Do you belong to a particular religion? (Circle yes or no only.)	YES NO	YES NO
Do you celebrate religious holidays because of your religion? (Circle yes or no only.)	YES NO	YES NO
Do you have an ethnic background? (Circle yes or no only.)	YES NO	YES NO
Do you have any ethnic celebrations at home? (Circle yes or no only.)	YES NO	YES NO
Were all your grandparents born in the U.S.? (Circle yes or no only.)	YES NO	YES NO
In what city will you live when you are 25?		
How many kids do you plan to have?		
What career will you work in?		

DAY 3   Today you will introduce students to the census data. Visit the U.S. Census Bureau at **www.census.gov**. Familiarize students with the site by selecting "2002 Data Profiles—ACS." To guide them, select "choose a state" at **www.census.gov/acs/www/Products/Profiles/Single/2002/ACS/index.htm** and select Arizona.

Have students use the Census Worksheet to summarize the information about Arizona.

Can the students draw any conclusions about the data they've just gathered? When everyone has completed the worksheet, allow them to browse the Census site to see the other types of information available.

DAY 4   Assign students to work in pairs. Assign each pair a state and capital city to research.

Explain that today students will work in pairs to gather information about an assigned state and its capital city. (Do not assign the state in which you reside. Pick states across the country for a good geographic sampling.) Students will use the State Worksheet to complete their tasks. Instruct them to:

- Use the U.S. Census Bureau site to gather the census information.
- Use **http://yellowpages.com** to gather information on religion (type in the city, state, and "religion").
- Use **google.com** to search for information on blue laws (for example, can underwear be sold on Sunday?). Have students search to see whether any blue laws exist for their assigned state.
- Use **google.com** to find a tourist information Web site for the capital city. Read through it and list the reasons why tourists would want to visit. Is the city full of history? Does it contain scenes important in the Revolutionary War, Civil War, or Indian Wars? Is it an agricultural haven? What is the history of the city? Why is it located where it is? Who settled it? What is the predominant claim to fame? For example, Phoenix, Arizona, is called the "Valley of the Sun," a name used to attract visitors from colder parts of the country.

DAY 5   Students will present their findings to the whole group. Which state was most populous? Which state had the highest number of males under age 45? Which state had the highest number of females over 45? Why? Have each pair provide an average number of people per church for their city. Where is the highest concentration of churches?

Who found blue laws? What were they? Is there any correlation between blue laws and the number of religious institutions?

Discuss the different historical reasons for the founding of various cities. Have students create a one-sentence summary of their city. For example, Phoenix, Arizona, the "Valley of the Sun," has more males than females, with an average age of 31, with 50% of the population in married households.

SECTION 2—RESOURCE UNITS

Census Worksheet

Visit the U.S. Census Bureau at **www.census.gov**. Select "2002 Data Profiles—ACS." Select "choose a state" and select Arizona. Use the following worksheet to summarize the information about Arizona.

ARIZONA CENSUS DATA

Total number of males	
Total number of females	
Males age 0–44 (round off and estimate)	
Males age 45+ (round off and estimate)	
Females age 0–44 (round off and estimate)	
Females age 45+ (round off and estimate)	
Median age	
Total households	
Married couple households	
Percentage with bachelor's degree or higher	
Median household money income	
Percentage of people below the poverty level	

HOW SOCIAL ARE WE ANYWAY?

DAY 6 Create a wall map of the geographic regions students have explored. Place the students' one-sentence summaries over their capital cities. Send students back to the Internet to explore your own state. Use the same steps covered in Day 4, and fill in the same worksheet, but this time for selected cities within your state. If you are in a large metropolitan area, select all the suburbs of the main city. If you are in a smaller town, select the capital and other populated areas to give a snapshot of the state.

DAY 7 Have students work in pairs to complete a written summary of their findings. Instruct them to be sure to include a table with the information they gleaned from Day 4 and Day 6 assignments. The summary must include conclusions the students have drawn from comparing and contrasting the census data for each city and state and tourist data they found. These summaries will be presented to the class at the end of the unit.

DAY 8 The class has used demographic and research data to draw conclusions. Now it's time to use online newspapers to research more about the city and state that were explored in Day 4. Using the newspaper link **http://azcentral.com**, students can browse the online editions of the *Arizona Republic* to discover local cultural issues. For example, November 1 in Phoenix, Arizona, is celebrated as Los Dias de los Muertos or the Day of the Dead. This is a Mexican tradition, and Phoenix has a high Mexican population. A search of the Arizona Republic online edition shows many events related to Mexican traditions, but common within the local culture. What other cultural customs can be discovered? What kinds of foods are common in the city? What languages are common in the city? Are Native American traditions apparent? What anomalies exist? (For example, Arizona has the highest per capita percentage of boat ownership in the U.S.)

DAY 9 Have students use an online newspaper for your local city and state to perform the same search as they did on Day 8.

DAY 10 Discuss the information found on your local area. What sorts of historical happenings influence your city? What kinds of cultural events form a frame for your year? Seaside in summer? Snowing in winter? As a class, determine what other information you need to provide a definitive picture of your area. Tell students that their goal over the weekend will be to interview two long-time residents of your area. Long-time residents are those who have lived in the area more than 30 years. As a class, select a list of questions that students will have answered. Be sure to consider the role of agriculture, industry, government, religion, and education.

DAY 11 Have students work in groups of four to summarize the results of their interviews. Then aggregate all the information into a whole from which data can be

State Worksheet

State _____   **Capital City** _____

Total number of males _____   Total number of males _____

Total number of females _____   Total number of females _____

Males age 0–44 _____   Males age 0–44 _____

Males age 45+ _____   Males age 45+ _____

Females age 0–44 _____   Females age 0–44 _____

Females age 45+ _____   Females age 45+ _____

Median age _____   Median age _____

Total households _____   Total households _____

Married couple households _____   Married couple households _____

Percentage with bachelor's degree or higher _____   Percentage with bachelor's degree or higher _____

Median household money income
_____

Median household money
_____

Percentage of people below the poverty level _____   Percentage of people below the poverty level _____

Blue Laws

Are there any existing blue laws?
_____
_____
_____

Are there any local quirks? Any local debates? (For example, residents of NYC worry about rent-controlled apartments.)
_____
_____
_____

Religion

Total number of churches in the yellow pages _____   Total number of churches in the yellow pages _____

Three most common denominations
_____
_____
_____

Three most common denominations
_____
_____
_____

extrapolated. What do long-time residents say about the local area? What brought them here? What keeps them here?

Compare your local data with the data you discovered about your assigned area. What types of lifestyles are representative for each area (based on your research)?

DAY 12 Summarize the lesson and offer some parting thoughts. Who lives where? What is their cultural influence? What types of food, religion, and history fill their days?

TEACHING TIPS Humans come equipped with notions and preconceived ideas. Many are reinforced by language choices. What do you call your noon meal? Supper? Dinner? Lunch?

Recall Pavlov's experiments, in which dogs would salivate at the sound of a bell. This is a learned reaction, similar to humans' learned reactions to language and behavior. Is it common to keep your house doors locked? Or are they locked only at night, or when you leave? Do you live in a gated community? What message might this send to folks who don't live there? Take a look at your refrigerator. Is it covered with magnets depicting your various travels? Is it covered with hand-drawn pictures or photographs? None of the above? What we choose to display, whether at home or in our classrooms, sends loud messages to our students. Some of the messages may be unintended.

When teaching these lessons, look for body language. Some students are extremely defensive about their cultural or sociological backgrounds. Don't forget that some students may not know anything about their backgrounds. Perhaps they are adopted, simply have never discussed backgrounds with their parents, or may not know who both parents are. Some students "adopt" a culture and join in various gangs. Each gang establishes their own cultural mores, and extreme rivalries can erupt over what the teacher may view as "nothing."

Keep the focus on the general, rather than the specific, to avoid conflict and reinforce the message of the unit. Be prepared to divulge pieces of your own background. (Think about it ahead of time, so that you know exactly what you will choose to divulge and what you will choose not to.) As you open the classroom discussions, be prepared for students to ask probing questions about virtually every aspect of your life. Again, decide what boundaries you will draw ahead of time. Check with your principal to see if there are any school board mandates about what can and cannot be discussed in a classroom.

Author's note: My students know my husband, children, and their spouses, and have seen pictures of my dogs and cats. I am continually asked about my views on children, discipline, and marriage. My personal religious views are not divulged, but religion is approached from a world view, especially with our continued conflicts in the Middle East. This gives a perfect launch for customs and cultures and how all sides believe they are doing the "right" thing.

LESSON EXTENDERS

Extend the student survey. Have students interview two teenagers who are not attending your school. Students will compare the answers with the other student responses.

Read poetry from the Harlem Renaissance, T. S. Eliot, Walt Whitman, and Maya Angelou. What themes are consistent through the poems? Develop a timeline of the 20th century based on these poets and others who you discover. What were the major issues in each decade?

Research religion. What are the top five religions worldwide? What are the top five religions in the U.S.? What are the top five religions in your community? Is there a dominant religion in your community, county, or state? Has this affected the rules and procedures that your school must follow?

Review the history of automotive plants in Michigan. What has happened to the communities that were built around the plants? Are they still communities? Draw conclusions about what went wrong. Review the copper industry in Arizona. What happened to Bisbee when the copper plant closed? What happened to Ajo when the copper plant closed? Compare and contrast these two cities with the Michigan cities you discover.

List the cities chosen in the surveys as where students will live at age 25. Research the cost of living for each city. Chart them. Are they similar? How? What conclusions can you draw?

Assessment

CRITERIA	1 UNSATISFACTORY	2 SATISFACTORY	3 EXEMPLARY	SCORE
SOCIAL STUDIES STANDARDS				
Understanding of culture, and how cultural systems generate thought processes and subsequent actions	Understanding is not in evidence.	Student demonstrates acceptable understanding within the context of this project.	Student demonstrates exemplary understanding, making connections to personal experience through higher level applications of thinking.	
Recognition of the ideas associated with individual human development and identity	Understanding is not in evidence.	Student demonstrates acceptable understanding within the context of this project.	Student demonstrates exemplary understanding, making connections to personal experience through higher level applications of thinking.	
Understanding of interactions among individuals, groups, and institutions	Understanding is not in evidence.	Student demonstrates acceptable understanding within the context of this project.	Student demonstrates exemplary understanding, making connections to personal experience through higher level applications of thinking.	
NETS				
Recognition of social, ethical, and human issues related to technology	Understanding is not in evidence.	Student demonstrates acceptable understanding within the context of this project.	Student demonstrates exemplary understanding, making connections to personal experience through higher level applications of thinking.	
Use of technology research tools	Student shows lack of minimum proficiency in using these tools.	Student meets minimum proficiency for using these tools.	Student goes beyond minimum proficiency for using these tools, applying their use beyond the requirements of this project.	
Use of technology problem-solving and decision-making tools	Student shows lack of minimum proficiency in using these tools.	Student meets minimum proficiency for using these tools.	Student goes beyond minimum proficiency for using these tools, applying their use beyond the requirements of this project.	
			Subtotal Points	

continued next page

SECTION 2—RESOURCE UNITS

Assessment

CRITERIA	1 UNSATISFACTORY	2 SATISFACTORY	3 EXEMPLARY	SCORE
RESEARCH				
Research content	Topic is vague. No clear major points are presented. There is little or no evidence to support the points.	Topic is presented in an appropriate fashion. There is evidence to support the major points. Facts are correct.	Product surpasses the expectations. Information is synthesized in insightful ways. Facts are correct, and additional research is presented to elaborate.	
Research resources	Student uses few assigned resources. Analysis is inaccurate.	Student uses assigned resources and presents accurate analysis of same.	Students uses more resources than are assigned. Student finds and presents additional valid resources to complement and enhance subject.	
Research quality	Topic is scattered. Facts are inaccurate.	Topic is presented in a logical and clear fashion. Point "A" leads to Point "B," and so on. Writing is clear.	Topic is skillfully and thoroughly discussed and synthesized in an original way. Writing is fresh and distinguished.	
Research usage and mechanics	Several deviations from standard English usage are evident.	Minor deviations from standard English usage are evident.	No deviations from standard English usage are evident.	
TEAMWORK				
Team collaboration	Student doesn't work with team. Student doesn't try. Student produces no or little acceptable work.	Student works with others on team (regardless of individual likes or dislikes). Student consistently participates in team course work, and satisfactorily completes all assignments.	Student facilitates group work—either as consensus leader or consensus maker. Student positively encourages other teammates and is looked to for advice.	
Team assignments	Team doesn't work together. Team produces no or little acceptable work.	Team works together (regardless of individual likes or dislikes). Team satisfactorily completes all assignments in a timely fashion.	Team works well together, utilizing each member's strengths. All students are engaged and working beyond requirements.	
INDIVIDUAL WORK				
Individual assignments	Student doesn't complete all assignments. The completed assignments are unacceptable.	Student completes all assignments in a satisfactory and timely manner.	Student completes assignments in a distinguished and intentional above-grade-level fashion. Assignments extend learning beyond the requirements and show evidence of synthesis of materials.	
Individual participation	Student does not participate in classroom assignments, or participation is disruptive, rather than constructive.	Student participates in classroom assignments in a satisfactory and constructive fashion.	Student participation is above satisfactory, and student extends classroom learning for other students.	
			Total Points	

An artist's map of the Middle East.

Virtual Reality, Cultural Reality: A Study of the Middle East

WALTER MCKENZIE

"The new electronic interdependence recreates the world in the image of a global village."

Marshall McLuhan

UNIT OBJECTIVES

Students will be challenged to:

- Examine the cultural, political, and military realities of the Middle East.
- Identify the leaders, resources, and issues of each Middle Eastern state.
- Identify a source of conflict for a specific state or group of states.
- Develop original graphics to represent the leaders, values, and resources of the state or states involved in the conflict.
- Craft a concept map that takes in all the possibilities for the resolution of the conflict.
- Create an interactive hypermedia presentation that requires the viewer to participate as a leader in making decisions to resolve the conflict, with multiple possible endings to the presentation.

SOCIAL STUDIES STANDARDS ADDRESSED

I **Culture**
Social studies programs should include experiences that provide for the study of culture and cultural diversity.

II **Time, Continuity, and Change**
Social studies programs should include experiences that provide for the study of the ways human beings view themselves in and over time.

III **People, Places, and Environments**
Social studies programs should include experiences that provide for the study of people, places, and environments.

VI **Power, Authority, and Governance**
Social studies programs should include experiences that provide for the study of how people create and change structures of power, authority, and governance.

IX **Global Connections**
Social studies programs should include experiences that provide for the study of global connections and interdependence.

NETS•S ADDRESSED

2 **Social, Ethical, and Human Issues**
- Students understand the ethical, cultural, and societal issues related to technology.
- Students develop positive attitudes toward technology uses that support lifelong learning, collaboration, personal pursuits, and productivity.

3 **Technology Productivity Tools**
- Students use technology tools to enhance learning, increase productivity, and promote creativity.

4 **Technology Communications Tools**
- Students use a variety of media and formats to communicate information and ideas effectively to multiple audiences.

5 **Technology Research Tools**
- Students use technology to locate, evaluate, and collect information from a variety of sources.
- Students use technology tools to process data and report results.
- Students evaluate and select new information resources and technological innovations based on the appropriateness to specific tasks.

6 **Technology Problem-Solving and Decision-Making Tools**
- Students employ technology in the development of strategies for solving problems in the real world.

VIRTUAL REALITY, CULTURAL REALITY: A STUDY OF THE MIDDLE EAST

CENTRAL DISCIPLINE AREA

Current Events

As high school students build a knowledge base of history, they gain a perspective in which to judge the contemporary political, cultural, and military conflicts of our era. The proper study of current events should be within the context of larger themes, trends, and values that serve as the filter for interpreting today's news. By helping students make connections between their own learning in the social studies and the situations that arise around them, teachers can provide skills that will last a lifetime as active participants as citizens of our nation and of the world.

UNIT DESCRIPTION

The Middle East continues to be a critical region of world politics, with implications for nations around the globe. In this unit students will study the recent history of nations within the Middle East and focus on a specific conflict currently in the news that requires an understanding in broad terms. Then students will create an interactive simulation that invites the viewer to make choices in the role of a world leader that have very real consequences for his or her nation. This virtual presentation will reflect student understanding of the complexity of international relations, global politics, and cultures.

Unit Tools

INTERDISCIPLINARY LINKS

Language Arts: Students will read and analyze information to gain a composite understanding of a specific nation and a current conflict it is experiencing.

Information Literacy: Students will analyze news sources for validity and accuracy.

Visual Arts: Students will create a graphic presentation reflecting their understanding of the cultures, politics, and potential resolutions to a specific conflict.

SPOTLIGHT ON TECHNOLOGY

Internet Research: Students will use the Web to access and analyze sources of information.

Graphics Editing: Students will create original graphics in GIF format that represent specific persons and events for their Flash movie.

Hypermedia: Students will create a hypermedia presentation consisting of buttons and internal links that allow the viewer to experience a virtual simulation of the resolution of a current event.

TECHNOLOGY RESOURCES NEEDED

Hardware
    computers with Internet access
    digital scanner

SECTION 2—RESOURCE UNITS

Software
Web browser
word processor
graphics editor
Inspiration
PowerPoint

WEB AND LITERATURE RESOURCES

Web Resources
Al Qaeda Training Manual: **www.usdoj.gov/ag/trainingmanual.htm**
Arab Media Internet Network: **www.amin.org**
Arab Net: **www.arab.net**
CIA World Fact Book: **www.cia.gov/cia/publications/factbook/**
Country Studies: **http://lcWeb2.loc.gov/frd/cs/cshome.html**
Foundation for Middle East Peace: **www.fmep.org**
Global Connections: **www.pbs.org/wgbh/globalconnections/**
Hot Spot: Iraq: **www.nationalgeographic.com/iraq/**
Iran Weekly Press Digest: **www.iranwpd.com**
Looking for Answers: **www.pbs.org/wgbh/pages/frontline/shows/terrorism/**
Middle East Information Network: **www.mideastinfo.com**
Middle East Network Information Center: **http://link.lanic.utexas.edu/menic/**
Middle East Newspapers: **www.refdesk.com/mideast.html**
MidEast Web: **www.mideastWeb.org**
New York Times International:
  www.nytimes.com/library/world/mideast/mideast-peace-index.html
Peace Process: **www.mfa.gov.il/mfa/go.asp?MFAH000c0**
Search for Peace Historical Documents:
  http://usembassy-israel.org.il/publish/peace/peaindex.htm
U.N. Information System on the Question of Palestine:
  http://domino.un.org/UNISPAL.NSF
U.S. State Department Background Notes: **www.state.gov/r/pa/ei/bgn/**

Literature Resources
Al Qaeda and What It Means to Be Modern, John Gray
The Arab Mind, Raphael Patai
The Crisis of Islam: Holy War and Unholy Terror, Bernard Lewis
Crusades Through Arab Eyes, Amin Maalouf
Guests of the Sheik: An Ethnography of an Iraqi Village, Elizabeth Warnock Fernea
The Israel-Arab Reader: A Documentary History of the Middle East Conflict, Walter Laqueur & Barry Rubin (Eds.)
The Jewish Mind, Raphael Patai
Modern Iran: Roots and Results of Revolution, Nikki R. Keddie
The New Iraq: Rebuilding the Country for Its People, the Middle East, and the World, Joseph Braude
Palestine and the Arab-Israeli Conflict, Charles D. Smith
Understanding Arabs: A Guide for Westerners, Margaret K. Nydell
What Everyone Needs to Know About Islam, John L. Esposito

VIRTUAL REALITY, CULTURAL REALITY: A STUDY OF THE MIDDLE EAST

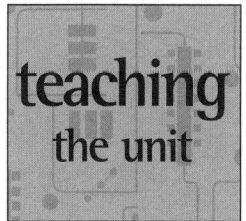

DAYS 1–3 Group students into teams of four or five and have them read online and hard copy sources on the Middle East.

Ask each group to identify a specific country and a conflict it is facing today. Students should gather political, religious, and cultural information on the nation or nations they select.

Have each group report back to the class at the end of Day 3.

DAY 4 Allow time for each group to further study the chosen topic through these news sources:

- Middle East Information Network: **www.mideastinfo.com**
- Middle East Network Information Center: **http://link.lanic.utexas.edu/menic/**
- Middle East Newspapers: **www.refdesk.com/mideast.html**
- MidEast Web: **www.mideastWeb.org**

Students may also use additional sources that are pertinent to their research, once they have these sources approved by the teacher.

DAYS 5–7 Have the same groups work to brainstorm all the possible resolutions to the conflict they are studying. This can include third parties that assist the country in question, positive outcomes, and outcomes that do not improve the quality of life for citizens.

Once the groups have exhausted their brainstorming, ask them to select four to six possible outcomes that are the most plausible given the current conditions in the Middle East.

DAYS 8–10 Have students use a graphics editor to design buttons in GIF format that represent significant persons and events in the conflict they are studying.

DAYS 11–13 Have students use Inspiration to create a concept map that begins with the conflict in its current condition and shows each of the possible outcomes for the conflict moving as a flowchart away from the conflict. They may import their original graphics as part of the map.

SECTION 2—RESOURCE UNITS

DAYS 14–16 Have students work in their groups to create a storyboard that shows each of the possible outcomes stated in their concept map. The storyboard should include a main menu of the conflict and its possible outcomes, along with separate frames for each outcome and its implications for the nation.

DAYS 17–19 Have students work in groups on interactive hypermedia presentations based on their storyboard, importing buttons and creating links from their buttons to each slide of possible outcomes. The presentation should contain navigation buttons that allow the viewer to return to the main menu slide at any point, and to make choices on each slide as to which course of action is best.

Navigation buttons should lead the viewer to slides that explain the cultural and political implications of their decisions and allow them the chance to return and reconsider their decision if they so choose.

DAY 20 Load each presentation on a computer and allow groups to circulate, participating in one another's simulations. Allow time for feedback and discussion at the end of the session.

TEACHING TIPS A hypermedia presentation should not be linear in nature; make sure students understand that the viewer should be able to jump from slide to slide at will without having to progress in a slideshow format.

Knowledge of graphics editing, Inspiration tools, and basic PowerPoint functions is important in supporting your students in this unit. To brush up on a specific application you use for graphics, Web pages, or PowerPoint, simply search using your favorite engine for tutorials for your products.

LESSON EXTENDERS Have your class Web page link to each of your hypermedia presentations.

Create a link from your school's main page to your class Web page.

Use student skills in creating digital graphics, semantic maps, and hypermedia presentations for new experiences in researching and understanding primary sources.

Assessment

CRITERIA	1 UNSATISFACTORY	2 SATISFACTORY	3 EXEMPLARY	SCORE
SOCIAL STUDIES STANDARDS				
Understanding of culture and cultural diversity	Understanding is not in evidence.	Student demonstrates acceptable understanding within the context of this project.	Student demonstrates exemplary understanding, making connections to personal experience through higher level applications of thinking.	
Understanding of time, continuity, and change	Understanding is not in evidence.	Student demonstrates acceptable understanding within the context of this project.	Student demonstrates exemplary understanding, making connections to personal experience through higher level applications of thinking.	
Understanding of people, places, and environments	Understanding is not in evidence.	Student demonstrates acceptable understanding within the context of this project.	Student demonstrates exemplary understanding, making connections to personal experience through higher level applications of thinking.	
Understanding of power, authority, and governance	Understanding is not in evidence.	Student demonstrates acceptable understanding within the context of this project.	Student demonstrates exemplary understanding, making connections to personal experience through higher level applications of thinking.	
Recognition of global connections and interdependence	Understanding is not in evidence.	Student demonstrates acceptable understanding within the context of this project.	Student demonstrates exemplary understanding, making connections to personal experience through higher level applications of thinking.	
NETS				
Recognition of social, ethical, and human issues related to technology	Understanding is not in evidence.	Student demonstrates acceptable understanding within the context of this project.	Student demonstrates exemplary understanding, making connections to personal experience through higher level applications of thinking.	
Use of technology productivity tools	Student shows lack of minimum proficiency in using these tools.	Student meets minimum proficiency for using these tools.	Student goes beyond minimum proficiency for using these tools, applying their use beyond the requirements of this project.	
Use of technology communications tools	Student shows lack of minimum proficiency in using these tools.	Student meets minimum proficiency for using these tools.	Student goes beyond minimum proficiency for using these tools, applying their use beyond the requirements of this project.	
Use of technology research tools	Student shows lack of minimum proficiency in using these tools.	Student meets minimum proficiency for using these tools.	Student goes beyond minimum proficiency for using these tools, applying their use beyond the requirements of this project.	
Use of technology problem-solving and decision-making tools	Student shows lack of minimum proficiency in using these tools.	Student meets minimum proficiency for using these tools.	Student goes beyond minimum proficiency for using these tools, applying their use beyond the requirements of this project.	
			Subtotal Points	

continued next page

SECTION 2—RESOURCE UNITS

Assessment

CRITERIA	1 UNSATISFACTORY	2 SATISFACTORY	3 EXEMPLARY	SCORE
OTHER CLASS WORK				
Research content and quality	Information is not screened for validity and accuracy.	Information comes from various recommended works and is screened for validity and accuracy.	Information is gathered from additional sources beyond basic recommended works and is screened for validity and accuracy.	
Concepts and understanding	Final work product contains fewer than four possible outcomes and does not demonstrate understanding of the political and cultural realities of the nation studied.	Final work product contains four to six possible outcomes and demonstrates understanding of the political and cultural realities of the nation studied.	Final work product contains more than six possible outcomes and demonstrates understanding of the political and cultural realities of the nation studied.	
Collaboration and participation	Student did not contribute as an active group member.	Student contributed as an active group member.	Student served as a leader for the group.	
Technical skill	Student used digital tools to create a linear presentation.	Student used digital tools to create a hypermedia presentation.	Student used digital tools to create an interactive hypermedia presentation.	
			Total Points	

A pollster poses survey questions to an interviewee.

Political Polling: Measuring Support for Environmental Policies

MATHEW MANWELLER

"Government, in the last analysis, is organized opinion. Where there is little or no public opinion, there is likely to be bad government."

MacKenzie King

UNIT OBJECTIVES

Students will be challenged to:

- Design and administer a political survey.

- Recognize biased questioning and understand the need for randomization.

- Collect and organize data, conduct statistical analysis of the data, and develop causal hypotheses based on the data.

- Use software to conduct histogram and simple regression analyses, and to present findings.

- Compare findings with those of other researchers who have conducted similar surveys.

SECTION 2—RESOURCE UNITS

SOCIAL STUDIES STANDARDS ADDRESSED

IV **Individual Development and Identity**
Social studies programs should include experiences that provide for the study of individual development and identity.

VI **Power, Authority, and Governance**
Social studies programs should include experiences that provide for the study of how people create and change structures of power, authority, and governance.

VII **Production, Distribution, and Consumption**
Social studies programs should include experiences that provide for the study of how people organize for the production, distribution, and consumption of goods and services.

VIII **Science, Technology, and Society**
Social studies programs should include experiences that provide for the study of relationships among science, technology, and society.

X **Civic Ideals and Practices**
Social studies programs should include experiences that provide for the study of the ideals, principles, and practices of citizenship in a democratic republic.

NETS•S ADDRESSED

3 **Technology Productivity Tools**
- Students use technology tools to enhance learning, increase productivity, and promote creativity.
- Students use productivity tools to collaborate in constructing technology-enhanced models, preparing publications, and producing other creative works.

4 **Technology Communications Tools**
- Students use telecommunications to collaborate, publish, and interact with peers, experts, and other audiences.
- Students use a variety of media and formats to communicate information and ideas effectively to multiple audiences.

5 **Technology Research Tools**
- Students use technology to locate, evaluate, and collect information from a variety of sources.
- Students use technology tools to process data and report results.
- Students evaluate and select new information resources and technological innovations based on the appropriateness to specific tasks.

6 **Technology Problem-Solving and Decision-Making Tools**
- Students use technology resources for solving problems and making informed decisions.
- Students employ technology in the development of strategies for solving problems in the real world.

POLITICAL POLLING: MEASURING SUPPORT FOR ENVIRONMENTAL POLICIES

CENTRAL DISCIPLINE AREA

Public Opinion

Public opinion is a growing field in the discipline of governmental studies. Political candidates, special interest groups, and consumer groups all use polling to persuade the public of certain policy prescriptions. However, like most data, survey data can be manipulated. Students need to understand how polls are conducted and how pollsters draw conclusions about the data collected.

UNIT DESCRIPTION

This unit introduces students to the field of public opinion and political polling. Students are asked to create a survey that focuses on attitudes toward environmental regulation. Students will draft a survey and then administer the survey to a randomly selected group of people. Afterward, they will organize and analyze the data in order to draw causal inferences about the effects of certain variables upon attitudes toward environmental legislation. Once they have developed some hypotheses, students will draft a report summarizing their findings, using graphs, charts, and statistical data to support their claims. The unit concludes with students researching other polling data on the same subject to determine whether their conclusions are similar to or different from the findings of other pollsters.

Unit Tools

INTERDISCIPLINARY LINKS

Mathematics: This unit introduces to students a variety of statistical concepts. Students will be asked to use a spreadsheet to determine mean, median, and mode values of respondent answers. They will also use spreadsheets to create histograms to identify the most common answers. Finally, students will conduct and interpret basic regressions of the data they collect.

Science: Students will need to do some research on polling with respect to attitudes about the environment. They will learn which environmental policies the public supports and which it opposes. Using the Web, students will study what other pollsters have concluded about public attitudes toward environmental regulation.

SPOTLIGHT ON TECHNOLOGY

Spreadsheets: Students will use spreadsheets to organize and analyze their data. Usually teachers use spreadsheets to organize data. This unit pushes students to use spreadsheets to develop higher order thinking skills. Teachers rarely use spreadsheets to conduct regression analysis. This unit allows students to interpret regression results without having to understand the complicated mathematics necessary to conduct regression analysis. Students will also use spreadsheets to convert data into easily understandable graphs and charts.

Handheld Devices or Laptops: Students will have the option of using handheld or laptop computers to collect their data. The portability of these technologies makes them ideal for work "in the field." Students may want to download their surveys into a handheld or laptop computer and then bring the hardware with them when they conduct their surveys.

SECTION 2—RESOURCE UNITS

Internet Research: Students will use the Web to search for other surveys about attitudes toward environmental legislation. They will compare their Web findings with their own research.

Web Forms: Advanced students can create on online survey that dumps data into a database for easy analysis.

TECHNOLOGY RESOURCES NEEDED

Hardware
computers with Internet access
handheld or laptop computers (optional)
digital video camera (optional)

Software
Web browser
spreadsheet software
word processing software
digital video editing software (optional)

WEB AND LITERATURE RESOURCES

Web Resources
Cast Your Vote: **www.learner.org/exhibits/statistics/**
Conservation Council of North Carolina:
    www.serve.com/ccnc/education/polling.shtml
Democracy Project: **www.pbs.org/democracy/**
Gallup Organization: **www.gallup.com**
Harris Poll Library: **www.louisharris.com/harris_poll/index.asp**
Kids Voting USA: **www.kidsvotingusa.org**
NES Guide to Public Opinion and Electoral Behavior:
    www.umich.edu/~nes/nesguide/nesguide.htm
On Politics Data Directory: **www.washingtonpost.com/**
    wp-srv/politics/polls/datadir.htm
PEW Research Center: **http://people-press.org**
Political Polling: From the Beginning to the Center of American Election
    Campaigns: **www.hbstaff.com/political.htm**
Polling Report: **www.pollingreport.com**
Polling: Through a Glass Darkly: **http://whyfiles.org/009poll/**
Public Agenda: **www.publicagenda.org**
Public Opinion Poll Question Database:
    www.irss.unc.edu/data_archive/pollsearch.html
Public Opinion Polls on the Internet:
    www.library.miami.edu/netguides/socopin.html
Roper Center: **www.ropercenter.uconn.edu**
Southeastern Coastal Policy Studies: **http://people.uncw.edu/jonesl/coastal.html**
The :30 Second Candidate: **www.pbs.org/30secondcandidate/**
U.S. Census Bureau Voting and Registration Data:
    www.census.gov/population/www/socdemo/voting.html
VoteMatch: **www.govote.com/Quiz.htm**
Zogby Polling: **www.zogby.com**

POLITICAL POLLING: MEASURING SUPPORT FOR ENVIRONMENTAL POLICIES

Literature Resources

Cartons, Cans, and Orange Peels: Where Does Your Garbage Go?, Joanna Foster

Eco-Nomics: What Everyone Should Know About Economics and the Environment, Richard Stroup

Grassroots of a Green Revolution: Polling America on the Environment, Deborah Lynn Guber

Introduction to Survey Research, Polling, and Data Analysis, Herbert Weisberg

Mobocracy: How the Media's Obsession With Polling Twists the News, Alters Elections, and Undermines Democracy, Matthew Robinson

The Next Step: 50 More Things You Can Do to Save the Earth, The Earthworks Group

Numbered Voices: How Opinion Polling Has Shaped American Politics, Susan Herbst

Polling and the Public: What Every Citizen Should Know, Herbert B. Asher

Silent Spring, Rachel Carson

Space Junk: Pollution Beyond the Earth, Judy Donnelly & Sydelle Kramer

State of the World 2003, Worldwatch Institute

The Voyage Begun, Nancy Bond

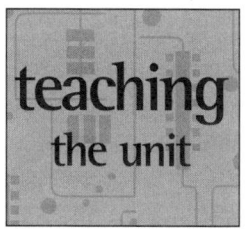

DAY 1

Students should be led in a brief discussion about why we use polls, who conducts polls, and how they are used to influence decision-making in government. Students should understand that polls are an instrument to understand the attitudes, feelings, and preferences of a large body of people. Polls are efficient because one can gain an understanding of how a large body of people feel about an issue, even though the pollster interviews only a small number of people.

Students should also be introduced to the difference between independent variables and dependent variables. Dependent variables are variables that measure the phenomenon you are interested in, such as: Are you liberal or conservative?; Are you for or against the death penalty?; How much do you like the Yankees? Independent variables are used to explain variation in dependent variables, such as gender, race, income, region, and age. Therefore, if students collect data on support for environmental legislation and gender, age, and region, they may conclude that support for the environment (dependent variable) is a function of how old the respondent is (independent variable) but not a factor of their gender (independent variable).

DAY 2 Students draft questions for their survey. This project focuses on support for or opposition to environmental legislation. Therefore, students are assigned some questions for their survey. The two questions students must ask are:

1. On a scale of 1 to 5 (1 being low and 5 being high), how much do you support legislation to protect the environment even if it means losing some jobs?

2. On a scale of 1 to 5 (1 being low and 5 being high), how much do you support legislation to protect the environment even if it means your (parent/spouse) will lose his or her job?

Students will also need to create a survey that asks about the respondent's gender, age, and political party affiliation. These will be their independent variables for this study.

Allow students to create some of their own questions too. These questions may be useful later in examining the effects of "biased" questions. For example, if they draft questions such as "Do you support the environment, or would you prefer that large corporations destroy all the land in America for greedy profit?" they will get different responses from those to the questions noted above.

When creating questions, it is important that students have a plan for recording answers in their spreadsheets. Spreadsheets will not add up "yes" and "no" responses, but they will add up 1s and 0s. Therefore, they need to code their verbal answers as numerical answers. For example, for the gender question, Female = 1 and Male = 0. Age can be coded as 0–15 (1), 16–30 (2), 31–45 (3), 46–60 (4), and so on. But what about political party affiliation? Spreadsheets can't record liberal or conservative, Republican or Democrat. In addition, there are strong conservatives and moderate conservatives. Your students will want to be able to record the variation. Therefore, I suggest creating a scale just like the questions about the environment listed above. For example, for the political affiliation question, students may want to ask, "On a scale of 1 to 10, 1 being the lowest and 10 being the highest, how liberal do you consider yourself?" It is a good idea to keep a separate paper or file indicating how your data are coded.

DAY 3 Once students have drafted their questions, they need to create an electronic or hard copy of their survey. Students may simply want to put their survey on paper and make copies to hand out to their respondents. Or, students may want to create an electronic version of their survey in a word processing program and put the survey on a laptop or a handheld computer. Regardless of how they administer the survey, all students will need to make a spreadsheet to organize their data, as in Figure 7. Students need one column for each question they ask. They should input only one answer per column.

DAYS 4–5 Students will need some time to conduct their surveys and collect their data. This may be done in a variety of ways. It may be most convenient to assign this part of the project as homework. Or the class may go on a field trip to a mall where there are lots of people. Or you may want to require students to conduct their interviews

POLITICAL POLLING: MEASURING SUPPORT FOR ENVIRONMENTAL POLICIES

FIGURE 7. Students use a spreadsheet program to organize their survey data.

	A	B	C	D	E	F	G
1	Answer to Quest 1	Answer to Quest 2	Gender (1=Female)	Age	Liberal (1=low, 10=high)		Score
2	4	1	0	2	8		1
3	2	3	0	4	3		2
4	1	3	0	5	2		3
5	5	1	0	2	7		4
6	3	2	0	3	6		5
7	3	3	0	2	7		
8	2	1	0	3	5		
9	3	4	0	4	4		
10	3	3	0	4	4		
11	5	5	0	1	8		
12	4	3	0	2	9		
13	5	4	0	2	8		
14	1	2	1	5	3		
15	2	2	1	3	4		
16	2	1	1	3	3		
17	1	5	1	5	2		

just before or after school. Regardless, students should be informed about the minimum number of interviews to conduct. The minimum should be 25, but 40 is preferable. Students should also be taught about the need for randomization. It may be helpful to lead a discussion about how selection bias may affect answers. For example, you may want to ask the class what might happen if they asked only their friends, only athletes, only adults, or only people from rural areas. This would be an excellent time to show the famous picture of President Truman holding the newspaper declaring "Dewey Defeats Truman." In that case, the Gallup organization polled only people with phones. At the time only wealthy people owned phones, so pollsters ignored the opinions of poorer Americans and the results turned out to be inaccurate.

DAY 6   Students will need a day to transfer all their data into the spreadsheet they created in Day 3.

DAY 7   Begin Day 7 by teaching basic spreadsheet data analysis skills. Students need to know how to create a histogram; compute averages, means, and modes; and run simple regressions. For Excel users, the Tools menu under Data Analysis offers a package of statistical tools, including "Descriptive Statistics" to determine mean, median, and mode. The package also offers a "Histogram" and "Regression" option.

DAY 8   Allow students time to conduct all their data analysis.

Student should start by conducting a descriptive statistics analysis of each dependent variable question. They should examine simple questions, such as the following:

- What was the average answer (1–5) to each question?
- What was the median answer (1–5) to each question?
- What was the mode answer (1–5) to each question?

Next, they will need to create histograms for all their dependent variable questions about the environment. The histograms will tell them which responses were the most common. You may also want to have students create histograms based on gender, age, and political affiliation (their independent variables). This will allow them to see how different groups answered the questions differently. (To organize the data by certain criteria, such as gender, use the Sort function in the Data menu.) It will help them understand how different groups may have different attitudes. The histograms in Figures 8 and 9 are based on the hypothetical data partially shown in Day 3. The graphs illustrate how the two genders answered (hypothetically) the first question differently.

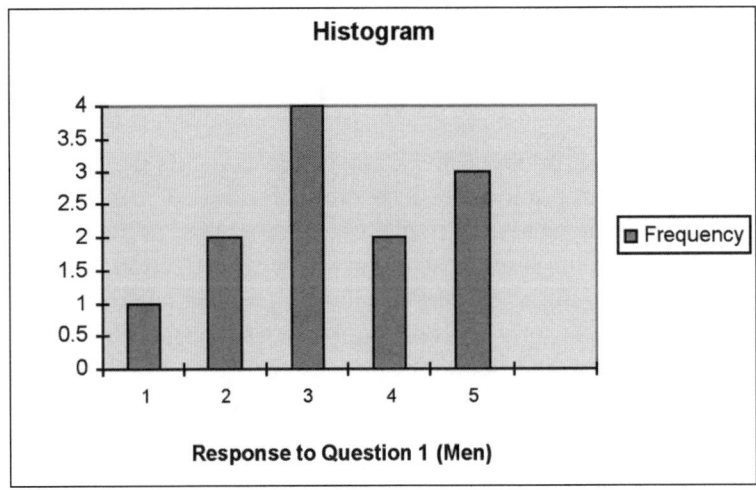

FIGURE 8. This histogram resulted from data analysis of survey question 1 (for men).

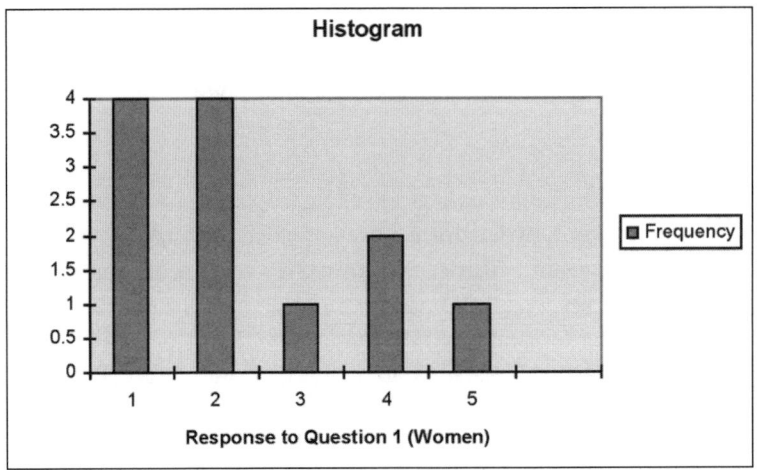

FIGURE 9. This histogram resulted from data analysis of survey question 1 (for women).

Last, students should do a regression analysis of their data. This is a lot simpler than it sounds. If using Excel, simply select the "Regression" option from the Data Analysis tools. When the dialogue box appears, place the cursor in the "Input Y Range" and highlight the column that holds the data for one of the dependent variables (one of the questions about the environment). Next, place the cursor in the "Input X Range" and then highlight all the columns that hold your independent variables (gender, age, political affiliation). Make sure the Labels and New Worksheet Ply boxes are checked. After you hit OK, you will get something that looks like Figure 10.

FIGURE 10. A regression analysis on the data can be done with a few clicks of the mouse.

	A	B	C	D	E
1	SUMMARY OUTPUT				
2					
3	*Regression Statistics*				
4	Multiple R	0.925924282			
5	R Square	0.857335776			
6	Adjusted R Square	0.836955173			
7	Standard Error	0.574364025			
8	Observations	25			
9					
10	ANOVA				
11		df	MS	F	Significance F
12	Regression	3	13.87741	42.0663	4.66E-09
13	Residual	21	0.329894		
14	Total	24			
15					
16		Coefficients	t Stat	P-value	Lower 95%
17	Intercept	3.169369512	2.232952	0.03657	0.217641497
18	Gender (1=Female)	-0.342061546	-1.36001	0.18825	-0.865114426
19	Age	-0.527252591	-2.36105	0.02797	-0.991656032
20	Liberal (1=low, 10=high)	0.280199351	2.044821	0.05361	-0.004767727

You and your students should ignore the section titled ANOVA. However, the top and bottom sections offer interesting insights for your students. The R Square value tells your students how much of the variance they can explain. In this example, I can say that gender, age, and political affiliation explain 85% of the difference in answers. The other 15% must be explainable by questions I did not ask. More important, students can look at the bottom of the report to see how the different variables affected answers. Noting that my Gender variable is -0.34, one can say, because the number is negative, that women were less likely to support environmental legislation (in reality, the opposite is true, but this is just hypothetical data). Looking at the Age variable of -0.52, one can say, because the number is negative, the older one gets, the less likely one is to support the environment. And last, looking at the Liberal variable, of .28, because it is positive, one can say that as one becomes more liberal, one is more likely to support the environment.

DAY 9 Students should write a report summarizing their findings using a word processing program. Students can cut and paste the graphs and charts from their spreadsheets into the document they are writing. The combination of written material with accompanying graphs and charts makes the publication more persuasive.

DAY 10 After students have summarized their conclusions, using the Web, they should research other polls about attitudes toward the environment (some sample Web sites have been provided in the Web Resources section). The process will allow students to compare their findings with those of other researchers.

As an optional assignment, students can go back and revise their essays. The revised essay would include their Internet research, explaining how their findings were similar to or different from what they found on the Web.

TEACHING TIPS Teachers need to have a general understanding of regression analysis if they are going to be able to answer some of the more complicated student questions. Specifically, a teacher may want to know the definitions of *t-stat* and *p-value*. It may be helpful to meet with a mathematics teacher before conducting this unit. Or, use the Help function in Excel to gain some information about these terms.

Teachers should also learn about the Sort and Histogram functions in Excel. The Sort function allows students to organize their data. For example, they may want to look only at the answers from young people. The Sort function will put all the data from young respondents on the top of the Excel sheet and group them together. In addition, to create a Histogram, students also need to create a Bin column. A Bin column tells the computer how many possible answers there are. For example, the example questions from this lesson had five possible answers (1–5). Therefore, I created a column in Excel that had the numbers 1 through 5 in it. The Histogram dialogue box will ask for Bin Range. Simply highlight your Bin column and insert.

LESSON EXTENDERS Students may want to create more complex surveys. They can ask other questions about attitudes toward the environment, probe for other demographic or explanatory (independent) variables, or simply draft a survey about completely unrelated political issues.

Students may want to submit their findings to a newspaper or local media outlet.

Students may wish to post their findings on a project Web site.

Students can write letters to local or national politicians using their findings as a basis for the letter.

Students may wish to submit their findings to a national polling organization and ask for feedback on their data and analysis in comparison with national norms.

Assessment

CRITERIA	1 UNSATISFACTORY	2 SATISFACTORY	3 EXEMPLARY	SCORE
SOCIAL STUDIES STANDARDS				
Understanding of individual development and identity	Understanding is not in evidence.	Student demonstrates acceptable understanding within the context of this project.	Student demonstrates exemplary understanding, making connections to personal experience through higher level applications of thinking.	
Recognition of how people create and change structures of power, authority, and governance	Understanding is not in evidence.	Student demonstrates acceptable understanding within the context of this project.	Student demonstrates exemplary understanding, making connections to personal experience through higher level applications of thinking.	
Understanding of how people organize for the production, distribution, and consumption of goods and services	Understanding is not in evidence.	Student demonstrates acceptable understanding within the context of this project.	Student demonstrates exemplary understanding, making connections to personal experience through higher level applications of thinking.	
Recognition of relationships among science, technology, and society	Understanding is not in evidence.	Student demonstrates acceptable understanding within the context of this project.	Student demonstrates exemplary understanding, making connections to personal experience through higher level applications of thinking.	
Understanding of the ideals, principles, and practices of citizenship in a democratic republic	Understanding is not in evidence.	Student demonstrates acceptable understanding within the context of this project.	Student demonstrates exemplary understanding, making connections to personal experience through higher level applications of thinking.	
			Subtotal Points	

continued next page

SECTION 2—RESOURCE UNITS

Assessment

CRITERIA	1 UNSATISFACTORY	2 SATISFACTORY	3 EXEMPLARY	SCORE
NETS				
Use of technology productivity tools	Student shows lack of minimum proficiency in using these tools.	Student meets minimum proficiency for using these tools.	Student goes beyond minimum proficiency for using these tools, applying their use beyond the requirements of this project.	
Use of technology communications tools	Student shows lack of minimum proficiency in using these tools.	Student meets minimum proficiency for using these tools.	Student goes beyond minimum proficiency for using these tools, applying their use beyond the requirements of this project.	
Use of technology research tools	Student shows lack of minimum proficiency in using these tools.	Student meets minimum proficiency for using these tools.	Student goes beyond minimum proficiency for using these tools, applying their use beyond the requirements of this project.	
Use of technology problem-solving and decision-making tools	Student shows lack of minimum proficiency in using these tools.	Student meets minimum proficiency for using these tools.	Student goes beyond minimum proficiency for using these tools, applying their use beyond the requirements of this project.	
SURVEY AND DATA				
Survey construction and use	Survey contains fewer than five questions, and the questions are confusing. Student polled fewer than 25 people.	Survey contains six or seven questions, and the questions are clear. Student polled between 25 and 35 people.	Survey contains eight or more clearly written questions. Student polled more than 35 people.	
Data analysis	Student fails to create histograms. Student is either unable to interpret the data or misinterprets the data and draws incorrect conclusions about public opinion.	Student creates histograms, but has trouble interpreting the data.	Student creates histograms and accurately interprets the data.	
Data reporting	Final report lacks a clear hypothesis, is poorly written, and fails to provide a clear summary of public opinion.	Final report has a hypothesis, but it is only marginally supported with data. Writing has limited grammatical errors.	Final report has a clear hypothesis, is well supported by a clear explanation of the data, and has no grammatical errors.	
			Total Points	

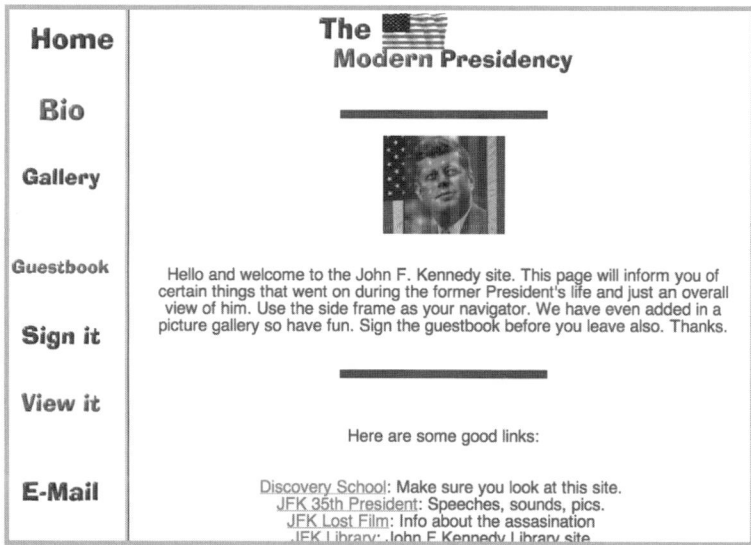

A student-created Web page.

The Modern Presidency

MICHAEL HUTCHISON

"The Presidency is the most powerful office in the Free World. Through its leadership can come a more vital life for our people. In it are centered the hopes of the globe around us for freedom and a more secure life. For it is in the Executive Branch that the most crucial decisions of this century must be made in the next four years..."

John F. Kennedy

UNIT OBJECTIVES

Students will be challenged to:

- Research the historic background of several U.S. presidents from the latter 20th century through the use of computer technology and cable television resources.

- Make and prove hypotheses about the effectiveness of each presidential administration.

- Use software and the Internet to collect, analyze, and report data.

- Develop a Web page or a multimedia slideshow that demonstrates the breadth of information learned.

SOCIAL STUDIES STANDARDS ADDRESSED

II **Time, Continuity, and Change**
Social studies programs should include experiences that provide for the study of the ways human beings view themselves in and over time.

V **Individuals, Groups, and Institutions**
Social studies programs should include experiences that provide for the study of interactions among individuals, groups, and institutions.

VI **Power, Authority, and Governance**
Social studies programs should include experiences that provide for the study of how people create and change structures of power, authority, and governance.

X **Civic Ideals and Practices**
Social studies programs should include experiences that provide for the study of the ideals, principles, and practices of citizenship in a democratic republic.

NETS•S ADDRESSED

3 **Technology Productivity Tools**
- Students use technology tools to enhance learning, increase productivity, and promote creativity.
- Students use productivity tools to collaborate in constructing technology-enhanced models, preparing publications, and producing other creative works.

4 **Technology Communications Tools**
- Students use a variety of media and formats to communicate information and ideas effectively to multiple audiences.

5 **Technology Research Tools**
- Students use technology to locate, evaluate, and collect information from a variety of sources.
- Students use technology tools to process data and report results.
- Students evaluate and select new information resources and technological innovations based on the appropriateness to specific tasks.

CENTRAL DISCIPLINE AREAS

United States History and Government

As President Kennedy noted in the opening quote, the office of president of the United States has a significant amount of power. It is instrumental not only in shaping domestic policy, such as Franklin D. Roosevelt's "New Deal," but in shaping foreign policy, as in the case of several U.S. presidents and their handling of the developing war in Vietnam. In this unit, students will be challenged to review the domestic and foreign policy accomplishments of eight presidents of the mid and late 20th century.

THE MODERN PRESIDENCY

UNIT DESCRIPTION
In this unit, students will develop PowerPoint presentations or Web pages highlighting the accomplishments of eight 20th century U.S. presidents. Working in small groups, students will research information about those presidents, including Franklin D. Roosevelt, Harry Truman, Dwight Eisenhower, John F. Kennedy, Lyndon B. Johnson, Richard M. Nixon, Jimmy Carter, and Ronald Reagan, which were featured in the 1997 *Assignment Discovery* series "The Modern Presidency." Students will collaborate on developing conclusions about the effect of the leadership of their assigned president on U.S. and world history.

Unit Tools

INTERDISCIPLINARY LINK
Language Arts: Students will utilize correct grammar and punctuation as they summarize their research about American presidents.

SPOTLIGHT ON TECHNOLOGY
Internet Research: Students will use the Web to collect data.

Web Pages: Students have the option to create Web pages to highlight the selected president.

Multimedia: Students have the option to create multimedia slideshows of the selected president.

TECHNOLOGY RESOURCES NEEDED
Hardware
   computers with Internet access
   scanner
   television with VCR
Software
   Internet browser
   presentation software (PowerPoint)
   HTML editor (such as Netscape Composer, Dreamweaver, or FrontPage)
   virtual work space such as Blackboard, TappedIn, or Yahoo! Groups (optional)

WEB AND LITERATURE RESOURCES
Web Resources
   The American Presidency: A Glorious Burden:
      http://americanhistory.si.edu/presidency/index.html
   The American Presidency: A Guide to Resources & Research on the Web:
      http://web.uccs.edu/history/ushistory/presidency.html
   The American President: **www.americanpresident.org**
   The American President: **www.pbs.org/wnet/amerpres/**
   American Presidents: Life Portraits: **www.americanpresidents.org**
   America Votes: Presidential Campaign Memorabilia From Duke Special
      Collections: **http://scriptorium.lib.duke.edu/americavotes/**
   Artful President:
      www.archivesofamericanart.si.edu/exhibits/presidents/presidents.htm

Blackboard: **http://company.blackboard.com**

By Popular Demand: **http://lcWeb2.loc.gov/ammem/odmdhtml/preshome.html**

China Today: **www.chinatoday.com**

A Chronology of U.S. Historical Documents: **www.law.ou.edu/hist/**

Discovery Channel School (contains supplemental lesson plans on presidents featured in the *Assignment Discovery* Modern Presidency series): **http://school.discovery.com**

Grolier Encyclopedia, Presidents: **www.grolier.com/presidents/**

The History Channel (includes sound files from 20th-century U.S. presidents): **www.historychannel.com**

The History Net: **www.thehistorynet.com/index.html**

Inaugural Addresses of the Presidents of the United States: **www.bartleby.com/124/**

Library of Congress: American Memory: **http://memory.loc.gov**

Michigan State University's Vincent Voice Library: U.S. Presidents of the 20th Century: **www.lib.msu.edu/vincent/presidents/index.htm**

Our Scandalous Presidents: Whom Would You Impeach?: **www.davison.k12.mi.us/dhs/staff/hewitt/scandals.htm**

PBS: The Presidents (contains supplemental information on presidents featured in the *The Presidents* series): **www.pbs.org/wgbh/amex/presidents/**

Portraits of the Presidents From the National Portrait Gallery: **www.npg.si.edu/exh/travpres/index6.htm**

Presidential Libraries Online: **www.archives.gov/presidential_libraries/addresses/addresses.html**

TappedIn: **http://ti2.sri.com/tappedin/**

Teacher Created Resource Page for the Modern Presidency: **www.vcsc.k12.in.us/staff/mhutch/modpres/mainpage.htm**

U.S. Presidents and the Presidency: **www2.worldbook.com/features/features.asp?feature=presidents&page=html/intro.htm&direct=no**

The White House: **www.whitehouse.gov**

Yahoo! Groups: **http://groups.yahoo.com**

Literature Resources

The American Heritage Illustrated History of the Presidents, Michael Beschloss (Ed.)

The American Presidency, Clinton Lawrence Rossiter

The American Presidency: A Glorious Burden, Lonnie Bunch

The American Presidency, An Interpretation, H. J. Laski

The American President: The Human Drama of Our Nation's Highest Office, Philip B. Kunhardt Jr., Philip B. Kunhardt III, & Peter W. Kunhardt

John F. Kennedy: An Unfinished Life, Robert Dallek

Keeping Faith, Jimmy Carter

The Modern American Presidency, Lewis Gould & Richard Norton Smith

The Modern Presidency, Nelson W. Polsby

The Modern Presidency: From Roosevelt to Reagan, John Hart

Presidential Anecdotes, Paul Boller

Presidential Power and the Modern Presidents, Richard E. Neustadt

Presidents: From Washington to Bush, Michael Beschloss

To the Best of My Ability, James McPherson (Ed.)

Truman, David McCullough

THE MODERN PRESIDENCY

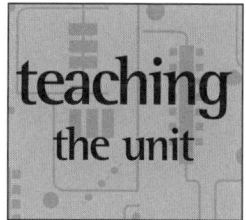

teaching the unit

DAY 1 — The teacher should introduce the powers of the presidency and present biographical sketches of those who have held the office. Generally, a good government or civics textbook will suffice in this task, although several of the listed Web sites will also provide information.

The teacher should also plan on this date to distribute materials related to the project, such as expectations, guidelines, and rubrics. The teacher may also wish to assign groups or have students assign themselves to a group (perhaps depending on the president they wish to research). As an alternative, the teacher may want to post all materials to a virtual work space, such as a class Internet site, a Web-based discussion group, or some other multi-user virtual environment.

The teacher may also wish to distribute "portfolios" (manila folders) to each student group to hold online resources they utilize. The teacher can gather these for evaluation, either for the briefing (see Day 8 and Days 9–10) or as part of the final project evaluation. If the teacher opts to use a virtual environment for collaboration and the archiving of data, digital portfolios can be created for each student or group.

DAY 2 — The teacher and class should brainstorm and reach a consensus on the criteria for identifying presidential success in the second half of the 20th century. In its final format this can be presented as a checklist or rubric. Each student should have a copy of the criteria in his or her hard or digital portfolio.

The teacher will also want to have students complete a library orientation regarding "traditional research" resources in addition to a virtual tour of Web-based research tools.

DAY 3 — The teacher will hold a guided practice on using a Web-page editor. If students are to complete multimedia slideshows instead, the teacher can offer a tutorial on using slideshow software.

DAYS 4–7 — Students should research their president and begin to develop storyboards for designing their Web page or multimedia slideshow.

DAY 8 — At the end of this class period, the teacher may wish to have students submit storyboards in their manila folders or digital portfolios. The purpose of this briefing is to ensure that students are complying with the guidelines set at the beginning of the project, as well as to check on any questions or concerns that students might have.

DAYS 9–10 Students complete the research phase of their project, as stated in the guidelines. The teacher will ask for another briefing at the conclusion of Day 10.

DAYS 11–13 Students will create their Web page or multimedia slideshow, using their research findings for content.

DAY 14 Students will submit their projects for final evaluation. The teacher may elect to make part of the evaluation process a group demonstration of the Web page or multimedia presentation, with the group showing the teacher and class their research.

TEACHING TIPS The teacher might wish to allot for one or two extra days for student collaborative work, simply to provide a cushion in case of some unexpected delay or obstacle (such as weather problem, school event, network breakdown, etc.).

The teacher may also wish for the groups to provide a written report on the president they researched.

The teacher may wish to consider several issues in preparation for the project. For example, you could add more recent presidents to the project since the time the original series aired.

In addition, because of the complexity of projects involving multimedia and Web design, it is recommended for the teacher to have a preliminary evaluation or briefing at the midpoint of the project to ensure that student groups are correctly following project guidelines.

It usually works well to have students assign themselves to groups rather than have the teacher do so, especially when the students are older. However, the teacher should remind students in advance that all the members of a group will be given the same score. It may be detrimental to a student's grade to join a group simply because it includes his or her friends.

LESSON EXTENDERS Ask students to do a comparison study of the various presidents in the unit based on their ability in foreign or domestic affairs, or a combination of the two. Use the established criteria to compare and contrast each chief executive.

Students might also research several presidents and have a "talk show" or roundtable debate in which the students acting as the presidents quiz each other regarding policies and decision making. A digital video recording of these events creates a meaningful record for authentic assessment.

Assessment

CRITERIA	1 UNSATISFACTORY	2 SATISFACTORY	3 EXEMPLARY	SCORE
SOCIAL STUDIES STANDARDS				
Understanding of time, continuity, and change	Understanding is not in evidence.	Student demonstrates acceptable understanding within the context of this project.	Student demonstrates exemplary understanding, making connections to personal experience through higher level applications of thinking.	
Understanding of interactions among individuals, groups, and institutions	Understanding is not in evidence.	Student demonstrates acceptable understanding within the context of this project.	Student demonstrates exemplary understanding, making connections to personal experience through higher level applications of thinking.	
Recognition of how people create and change structures of power, authority, and governance	Understanding is not in evidence.	Student demonstrates acceptable understanding within the context of this project.	Student demonstrates exemplary understanding, making connections to personal experience through higher level applications of thinking.	
Understanding of thte ideals, principles, and practices of citizenship in a democratic republic	Understanding is not in evidence.	Student demonstrates acceptable understanding within the context of this project.	Student demonstrates exemplary understanding, making connections to personal experience through higher level applications of thinking.	
NETS				
Use of technology productivity tools	Student shows lack of minimum proficiency in using these tools.	Student meets minimum proficiency for using these tools.	Student goes beyond minimum proficiency for using these tools, applying their use beyond the requirements of this project.	
Use of technology communications tools	Student shows lack of minimum proficiency in using these tools.	Student meets minimum proficiency for using these tools.	Student goes beyond minimum proficiency for using these tools, applying their use beyond the requirements of this project.	
Use of technology research tools	Student shows lack of minimum proficiency in using these tools.	Student meets minimum proficiency for using these tools.	Student goes beyond minimum proficiency for using these tools, applying their use beyond the requirements of this project.	
			Subtotal Points	

continued next page

Assessment

CRITERIA	1 UNSATISFACTORY	2 SATISFACTORY	3 EXEMPLARY	SCORE
PRESENTATION				
Speaking	Speaker is difficult to understand. Serious grammatical errors are evident.	Voice is clear. Some minor grammatical errors are evident.	Voice is clear and easy to understand. Correct grammar is used.	
Use of technology	Student demonstrates lack of mastery of technology, which negatively affects the effectiveness of the presentation.	Student demonstrates proficient use of technology. The use of technology increases the effectiveness of the presentation.	Student demonstrates exemplary use of technology. The use of technology significantly increases the effectiveness of the presentation.	
Length of presentation	Either the presentation does not meet the time requirement as specified in the guidelines or the use of time is not effective.	Presentation meets time requirements as set in the guidelines and includes the effective use of resources.	Presentation meets time requirement set in the guidelines, but also includes quality use of time in regard to the information and resources demonstrated.	
Response to questions	Student is unable to answer questions regarding the project, or the answers are incomplete.	Student is proficient in answering questions concerning the project.	Student demonstrates confidence in answering questions regarding the project.	
PROJECT				
Project design	Project does not include a storyboard or the portfolio is missing evidence of the planning process.	Project includes a storyboard and a portfolio documenting the planning process.	Project includes a storyboard, a portfolio documenting the planning process, and evidence of thorough research on the assigned president.	
Project formatting	Project is hard to navigate, and has illegible text and/or distracting graphics and special effects.	Project has simple navigation and legible text. Layout graphics do not distract from the presentation of content.	Project has intuitive navigation and legible text. Layout graphics enhance the presentation of content.	
Project creativity	Student uses graphics without attributing sources or lacks a follow-up task that invites the audience to extend their understanding of the content.	Student uses graphics with the proper citation of sources and includes at least one activity that invites the audience to complete a content-related task on- or offline.	Student uses original graphics and interactive features that challenge the audience to use the site content meaningfully online.	
Project requirements	The group did not follow directions including elements listed in the guidelines.	The group followed directions including most elements listed in the guidelines.	The group followed directions including all elements listed in the guidelines.	
Project accuracy	The facts presented include inaccuracies and do not include proper documentation.	The facts presented are accurate with some proper documentation.	The facts presented are accurate and include proper documentation with embedded links where appropriate.	
Mastery of content	Student demonstrates a lack of knowledge of the project subject.	Student demonstrates effective mastery of the project subject.	Student demonstrates exemplary mastery of content of the project subject.	
			Total Points	

THE MODERN PRESIDENCY

Additional Resources

The following pages provide samples of materials to use in this project.

RESOURCE PAGE   Create a page on your school's Web site to direct students to additional resources. Then, when the unit is completed, have students submit their Web pages to the school site. Figure 11 shows a resource page for one class.

FIGURE 11. Example of a teacher-created resource page.

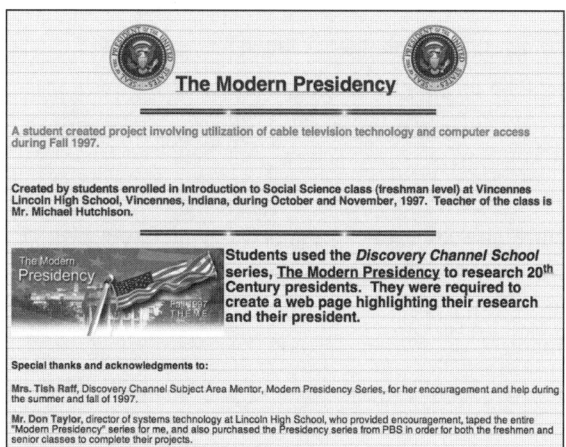

The Modern Presidency
Requirements for the Web Page

Each group must develop a Web page about the president they selected to research. The Web page must include the following components:

- _____ 1. At least two pictures of the assigned president, one of which will be a "mug shot" to be placed at or near the top of the Web page.
- _____ 2. At least two pictures of some event that occurred during the president's term of office.
- _____ 3. A biographical section regarding the president's life.
- _____ 4. A section that highlights the president's administration.
- _____ 5. At least three external links discussing the president. (External links refer to those links that lie outside the group's page.)

- Students are encouraged to utilize any resources or expertise they have at their disposal in creating pages. Examples of this expertise would include using Java script, frames, Web counters, graphics, sound files, and any other resources that are suitable and acceptable to the student group, teacher, and school technology department.

- All Web pages will be stored on the school Web server and will be available to anyone with Web access.

- Deadline dates have been set. Web pages are due on that date or before, without exception. Student groups may, if desired, turn in a Web project prior to the due date for a preliminary evaluation. Upon completion of that evaluation, the group may elect to accept their preliminary grade as the final grade or attempt to receive a higher grade by correcting whatever faults, if any, the teacher should find.

- All pages should be stored on disk. Each group is expected to contribute as many disks as necessary to store all the graphics, sound files, and other project elements. Disks may be brought from home or may be purchased.

- All completed entries and disks will become the property of the teacher upon submission until they are released.

- Students will be assessed according to an evaluation sheet to be created at a later date. However, criteria will include the following areas: creativity, historical accuracy, and adherence to the Web page construction requirements stated above. Other categories may be added to the final evaluation form. Students are reminded that all students in the group will be awarded the same grade.

- The total number of possible points for this project is 70.

- Students with questions about this project are encouraged to speak to the teacher as soon as possible.

The Modern Presidency
Requirements for the Multimedia Slideshow

Each group must develop a Microsoft PowerPoint presentation about the president they selected to research. This presentation should be a minimum of three minutes in length, including transitions.

Final presentations should include the following:

_____ 1. A title slide with each member of that group listed (using full names). The title slide should also include the name of the president the group researched.

_____ 2. At least three sound files, one of which should be an audio clip of that president speaking.

_____ 3. At least four pictures within the presentation, with at least one being a photo of the president who is the subject of the presentation. This picture should be included on the title slide.

_____ 4. A biographical sketch of the president, the accomplishments and failures, if any, of that president's administration, and information about that president after he left office (if applicable).

_____ 5. A final slide listing all the sources the group used in creating their presentation (bibliographical information).

Each student is required to participate in this project. This includes each student in each group contributing at least one 3-inch, high-density disk to help store the group's presentation. These may be brought from home or purchased.

Each group will be provided a manila folder in which they are to store the following items:

_____ 1. All storyboards the group used to develop the presentation.

_____ 2. Hard copies of all research done, either printed from the Internet or photocopied.

_____ 3. Rough copies of all work related to the textual composition.

_____ 4. Laser-printed copies of thumbnails of each slide.

In addition, each group is to submit a copy of its finished presentation on disk at the conclusion of the project. This is to be stored using the Pack and Go function found in the File menu in PowerPoint.

All finished presentations will become the property of the teacher. No projects will be returned to students until they are released by the teacher.

Consider the following evaluation notes:

- The finished project will include a completed portfolio (manila folder) and a PowerPoint presentation on disk.
- The maximum presentation value is 70 points.
- Portfolios may be collected and evaluated prior to the due date for the project.
- Each student in the group will be awarded the same score.
- Each group will be graded according to criteria to be developed at a later date. However, criteria will most likely include: quality of the portfolio, creativity, length of presentation, and adherence to the project requirements.
- The deadline date has been set. Presentations are due on that date, or before, without exception. Students may turn in a presentation prior to the due date for a preliminary evaluation. The group members may elect to accept the preliminary grade as their final grade or to make any suggested changes in order to increase their total score.
- Students should be aware that some project work will need to be completed outside of class time.
- This set of requirements may be updated as the class continues the project. Look for further updates.

The Modern Presidency
Web Page Evaluation Sheet

Name of group (president researched): _____

Full names of all group members: _____

_____

Evaluation Criteria

1. Web Page Construction
   (How did the group create their Web page? Do the links work? Is the text readable and formatted correctly? Do the graphics load correctly?)
   15 points maximum

   Group grade: _____ points

2. Creativity
   (What did the group do to develop a unique project? This includes providing pictures, creating an e-mail address, and using graphics such as animations and self-created visuals.)
   15 points maximum

   Group grade: _____ points

3. Project Requirements
   (Did the group follow directions for creating links on the page, listing their names on the page, placing pictures of their group's president on the page, and so on?)
   20 points maximum

   Group grade: _____ points

4. Historical Accuracy
   (Are the facts regarding the president accurate? Did the group complete sufficient research in creating the Web page?)
   10 points maximum

   Group grade: _____ points

5. Special Criteria
   (Special criteria include any effort made by the group to go above and beyond the basic requirements of the assignment, such as noticeable work done beyond class time, extensive research, and any other work deemed deserving of an award.)
   10 points maximum

   Group grade: _____ points

Final Evaluation Score (Addition of 1–5 above.)
   70 points total

   Group grade: _____ points

   Group letter grade: _____

Instructor Comments: _____

_____

The Modern Presidency
Multimedia Slideshow Evaluation Sheet

Name of group (president researched: _____

Full names of all group members: _____

_____

Evaluation Criteria

1. Portfolio Completion
   (A complete portfolio includes storyboards, thumbnails, and a hard copy of the resources used.)
   15 points maximum

   Group grade: _____ points

2. Presentation Length
   (The presentation runs within the assigned time range.)
   5 points total

   Group grade: _____ points

3. Creativity
   (What did the group do to develop a unique project? This includes the creative use of pictures, sound clips, and other forms of media.)
   25 points total

   Group grade: _____ points

4. Presentation Requirements
   (Did the group include a title slide, presidential sound clips, pictures, a bibliography, and the other requirements listed in the handouts?)
   20 points total

   Group grade: _____ points

5. Special Criteria
   (Special criteria include any effort made by the group to go above and beyond the basic requirements of the assignment, such as noticeable work done beyond the class time, extensive research, and any other work deemed deserving of a special reward.)
   5 points total

   Group grade: _____ points

Final Evaluation Score (Addition of 1–5 above.)
   70 points total

   Group grade: _____ points

   Group letter grade: _____

Instructor Comments: _____

A British stamp issued in 1982 to honor Charles Darwin for his contributions to geology and Galapagos Islands research.

All the World in an Archipelago

CYNDY JONES WOODS

"Nothing before had ever made me thoroughly realise, though I had read various scientific books, that science consists in grouping facts so that general laws or conclusions may be drawn from them."

Charles Darwin

UNIT OBJECTIVES

Students will be challenged to:

- Research and articulate why people have located in different places and environments.

- Categorize and distinguish various landforms and their influence on groupings.

- Examine the availability of resources.

- Theorize how geographic, social, cultural, and political influences may affect the future of the Galapagos Archipelago, and by extension, the future of our own areas.

- Effectively use geographic representations to acquire, process, and report information.

- Distinguish between physical and human characteristics of places.

- Analyze how human and physical systems interact with the environment.

- Examine and discuss the distribution of resources.

- Formulate and propose solutions for some of the discovered problems.

SECTION 2—RESOURCE UNITS

SOCIAL STUDIES STANDARDS ADDRESSED

III People, Places, and Environments
Social studies programs should include experiences that provide for the study of people, places, and environments.

V Individuals, Groups, and Institutions
Social studies programs should include experiences that provide for the study of interactions among individuals, groups, and institutions.

VII Production, Distribution, and Consumption
Social studies programs should include experiences that provide for the study of how people organize for the production, distribution, and consumption of goods and services.

IX Global Connections
Social studies programs should include experiences that provide for the study of global connections and interdependence.

NETS•S ADDRESSED

2 Social, Ethical, and Human Issues
- Students understand the ethical, cultural, and societal issues related to technology.
- Students practice responsible use of technology systems, information, and software.
- Students develop positive attitudes toward technology uses that support lifelong learning, collaboration, personal pursuits, and productivity.

5 Technology Research Tools
- Students use technology to locate, evaluate, and collect information from a variety of sources.
- Students use technology tools to process data and report results.
- Students evaluate and select new information resources and technological innovations based on the appropriateness to specific tasks.

6 Technology Problem-Solving and Decision-Making Tools
- Students use technology resources for solving problems and making informed decisions.
- Students employ technology in the development of strategies for solving problems in the real world.

CENTRAL DISCIPLINE AREA

People, Places, and Environments

People settle in places of opportunity with encouraging environments. Over time, opportunities change, often changing the environment as well. Changes can be positive, neutral, negative, or a combination. Because the Galapagos Archipelago is a contained ecosystem, these changes are readily noticed. Students will study the Galapagos Archipelago as a microcosm of the environmental changes wrought by people over time throughout the world.

UNIT DESCRIPTION This unit challenges students to observe and evaluate different belief systems that are intrinsic to human society—systems that often cause tension and conflict, and illustrate the continual need to adapt to economic, cultural, and environmental changes in our dynamic world.

The unit can be used in total or broken into parts. Individual lessons can be taught as standalone units, or used consecutively, to:

- enhance geographic knowledge of maps, spatial indicators, and landforms.
- learn about the Galapagos Archipelago.
- recognize and label different landforms and investigate how they affect humans and the distribution of ecosystems on earth.
- recognize and label resources and investigate how they affect humans and the distribution of ecosystems on earth.
- categorize and elaborate how geographic, social, cultural, and political influences may affect the future of the Galapagos Archipelago, and by extension, the future of our own areas.
- examine and analyze the movement of goods and services, and how this affects the environment.

Unit Tools

INTERDISCIPLINARY LINK *Language Arts:* Students will prepare a summary report for each unit that discusses their findings. Information from research will be incorporated, as well as anecdotal information gathered from online sources. The units will require the use of a large number of Web sites, graphs, maps, and data, as well as a significant amount of reading.

SPOTLIGHT ON TECHNOLOGY *Internet Research:* Students will use the Internet to find and read maps, and to learn about the Galapagos Archipelago, landforms, resources, ecosystems, and environmental issues. They will use the Internet to identify trends, collect anecdotal evidence, view culture presentations, and gather historical information.

Word Processing: Students will use word processing software to generate reports and graphs.

TECHNOLOGY RESOURCES NEEDED **Hardware**
  computers with Internet connections
  printer

SECTION 2—RESOURCE UNITS

> video presentation system
> digital camera
>
> **Software**
> word processing program
> presentation software

WEB, LITERATURE, AND VIDEO RESOURCES

Web Resources

Center for Educational Technologies and Classroom of the Future:
   www.cotf.edu/ete/modules/msese/earthsysflr/biomes.html

CIA: The World Factbook:
   www.cia.gov/cia/publications/factbook/docs/profileguide.html

Classroom of the Future Adaptation:
   www.cotf.edu/ete/modules/msese/earthsysflr/adapt.html

Construction Land: **www.constructionlandonline.com**

Cranford County: **http://storm.simpson.edu/~proctorn/croatan/**

Darwin Correspondence Online Database:
   http://darwin.lib.cam.ac.uk/perl/nav?class=place&term=Galapagos%20Archipelago&dmode=dr

David Levine's World Clock: **www.ibiblio.org/lunarbin/worldpop**

Dr. Richard Rothman's Galapagos Site:
   www.rit.edu/~rhrsbi/GalapagosPages/Galapagos.html

The Islands: Cornell University:
   www.geo.cornell.edu/geology/GalapagosWWW/GalapagosMap.html

Maps and Globes: **www.mcwdn.org/MAPS&GLOBES/LandForms.html**

National Geographic Map Machine:
   www.nationalgeographic.com/wildworld/terrestrial.html

PBS: Destination: Galapagos Islands:
   www.pbs.org/safarchive/5_cool/galapagos/g1_welcome.html
   Geography and Geology:
   www.pbs.org/safarchive/5_cool/galapagos/g22_geo.html
   Natural Selection:
   www.pbs.org/safarchive/5_cool/galapagos/g48_glossary.html#more
   Weather: **www.pbs.org/safarchive/5_cool/galapagos/g24_weather.html**
   Wildlife: **www.pbs.org/safarchive/5_cool/galapagos/g23_biology.html**

PBS: Evolution: Frequently Asked Questions:
   www.pbs.org/wgbh/evolution/library/faq/cat01.html#Q01

Population Reference Bureau:
   www.prb.org/Content/NavigationMenu/PRB/Educators/Human_Population/Environment4/Environment_Q_and_A1.htm

Sea Cucumbers: Charles Darwin Foundation:
   www.darwinfoundation.org/marine/FAQcuke.html

U.S. Census Bureau Foreign Trade Statistics: **www.census.gov/foreign-trade/www/**

U.S. Census Clock: **www.census.gov/cgi-bin/ipc/popclockw**

U.S. Geological Survey:
   http://mac.usgs.gov/mac/isb/pubs/MapProjections/projections.html#globe

ALL THE WORLD IN AN ARCHIPELAGO

Literature Resources
Evolution's Workshop: God and Science on the Galapagos Islands, Edward J. Larson
Flowering Plants of the Galapagos, Conley K. McMullen
Galapagos, A Natural History (2nd ed.), Michael H. Jackson
Galapagos: Islands Born of Fire, Tui De Roy
The Galapagos Islands: A Natural History Guide (6th ed.), Pierre Constant
The Galapagos Islands: The Essential Handbook for Exploring, Enjoying and Understanding Darwin's Enchanted Islands, Marylee Stephenson
Galapagos Wildlife, James Kavanaugh
A Guide to the Birds of the Galapagos Islands, Isabel Castro & Antonia Phillips
An Identification Guide to the Birds, Mammals, and Reptiles of the Galapagos Islands, Andy Swash, Robert Still, & Ian Lewington
Into Wild Galapagos, Elaine Pascoe (Ed.)
Lonely Planet Ecuador & the Galapagos Islands (6th ed.), Rob Rachowiecki & Danny Palmerlee
Lonesome George, Jean Craighead George
The Origin of Species, Charles Darwin (Also online at **www.literature.org/authors/darwin-charles/the-origin-of-species/**)
Reef Fish Identification: Galapagos, Paul Humann (Ed.)
The Voyage of the Beagle, Charles Darwin (Also online at **www.literature.org/authors/darwin-charles/the-voyage-of-the-beagle/chapter-17.html**)
Wildlife of the Galapagos, Julian Fitter

Video Resources
Galapagos Islands: Land of Dragons (National Geographic)

UNIT 1: GEOGRAPHY, LANDFORMS, AND RESOURCES

DAY 1 On the first day, encourage students to observe life around them and to wonder how we "see" and "map" the world. Begin with a writing exercise. Have the students write six guided statements about where they live. Write the following prompts on the board, and ask students to finish them.

> I live in (city/state/country).
>
> I live where telephone service to my dwelling (is/is not) available.
>
> I live in the (Northern/Southern Hemisphere).
>
> I live in a (desert/forest/coastal area/mountain zone).
>
> I live at _____ feet above/below sea level.
>
> I share my living space with _____ other humans.

Collect the answers, and discuss the "norm" in your area. (For example, telephone service in the Galapagos Islands is extremely limited, so it is not normal for families to have home telephone service. Likewise, it is common for many people to share a single dwelling.) Focus the students on the idea of resource availability in your particular area.

Using a wall map, point to your physical location, identifying the Northern and Southern Hemispheres, and any particular biomes (forest, coastal, desert, mountainous) you wish to draw attention to.

Ask students to identify the most prominent landforms within your physical area. Are these common to all areas? What are the common animals in your area? What are the common plants? How much annual rainfall does your area receive?

Introduce the homework assignment (see the following page). The students will be interviewing two high school students—not in your class—and reporting the findings on the following day. The interviewees are to remain anonymous. The information will be aggregated on Day 2.

DAY 2 In groups of four, students will tally the data from their interviews. Then, tally all the information on the board. Ask students whether they see any trends. For example, one trend response might be that Africa is a jungle. Is this really true? How would you discover this? What kind of map would show this information?

Have students begin their Web research at the U.S. Geological Survey site (**http://mac.usgs.gov/mac/isb/pubs/MapProjections/projections.html#globe**). Have students answer the following questions (which will help to establish their reading and information synthesizing ability):

- Why would you use a Mercator projection? (A Mercator projection is used to navigate or map equatorial regions.)
- What is the range of true distance on the Mercator map? (True distance ranges from 15N to 15S, but it is most precise at the equator.)
- Where on a Mercator map is distortion the least? (At the equator.)
- What makes the Robinson map unique? (The Robinson map offers a better balance of size and shape of high latitude lands. The scale is true at 38N and 38S.)
- What is an azimuth? (The azimuth is the angle measured in degrees between a base line radiating from a center point and another line radiating from the same point. Normally, the base line points north, and degrees are measured clockwise from the base line.)
- What's the use of a map projection? (A map projection is a systematic representation of a round body such as the Earth or a flat [plane] surface. Each map projection has specific properties that make it useful for specific purposes.)
- Which map projection would show less distortion of Greenland? (Robinson)
- Which map projection is in our classroom? (Answers will vary.)

Day 1 Homework Assignment

Ecoregions Interview Sheet

QUESTION	INTERVIEWEE ONE	INTERVIEWEE TWO
Where were you born?		
If you were not born here, why did you move here?		
How do you categorize this area (desert, mountains, coastal, river way)? What landforms are common in this area?		
If you could live anywhere, where would it be? Why?		
Where are the Galapagos Islands?		
What kind of landform do you think of when I say "Africa"?		
What kind of landform do you think of when I say "India"?		
What kind of landform do you think of when I say "Iceland"?		
What kind of landform do you think of when I say "Brazil"?		
What kind of landform do you think of when I say "Japan"?		

Directions: Ask two interviewees these questions, and carefully record their responses.

Now visit the National Geographic Map Machine (**www.nationalgeographic.com/wildworld/terrestrial.html**). In the remaining time, have students browse this map and list five different ecoregions they discover. Direct them to note the description of each.

DAY 3   Recall Day 2's exercise about ecoregions. Ask students whether they noticed any similarities regarding location. Does Japan have the same ecoregions as Africa? Why or why not?

What are the prominent landforms for each ecoregion?

Using the Maps and Globes Web site (**www.mcwdn.org/MAPS&GLOBES/LandForms.html**), students will write the definitions for these terms and answer the following questions:

continent	cape
volcano	isthmus
mountain	valley
plain and plateau	canyon
island	cliff
peninsula	swamp

- Which of these are found in your area? (Unless they live on a houseboat, all students should at least indicate that they live on a continent or an island.)
- How are ecoregions distributed? Why? (Is there a big ecoregion distributor in your neighborhood?)

Have students visit the Center for Educational Technologies and Classroom of the Future site (**www.cotf.edu/ete/modules/msese/earthsysflr/biomes.html**) to discover the six basic ecoregions of the world. Ask them to fill out the chart on the following page.

DAY 4   Recall Day 3's discussion of ecoregions and their distribution. Do ecoregions stay the same? What happens when humans move into an ecoregion?

Visit the Classroom of the Future Adaptation site at **www.cotf.edu/ete/modules/msese/earthsysflr/adapt.html**. Have students read the information and answer the following questions:

- What is an environment? (An environment includes all things and conditions found in a location.)
- What are the nonliving things of an environment? (Nonliving things of an environment include mountains, valleys, rivers, streams, rocks, soils, and climate.)

Day 3 In-Class Assignment
Six Basic Ecoregions of the World

Directions: List the six basic ecoregions of the world, describing what the landforms look like and including examples of typical plant and animal life in each.

ECOREGION	DESCRIPTION	LANDFORMS	PLANTS/ANIMALS

- Name three physical environments on earth. (Physical environments include dry with hard soils, wet with thick soils, hot, cold, hilly, flat, underwater, rocky, running water, and ice.)
- What is California west of the San Andreas fault doing? (It is being carried northward by the movement of the Pacific Plate.)
- What is the difference between natural and man-made changes? (Man-made changes occur in relatively short periods of time.)
- How can we see physical adaptations? (We can compare the skeletons of different animals.)

- What do the bat, human, bird, and horse have in common? (According to evolutionary theory, they descended from a common four-limbed ancestral species that lived hundreds of millions of years ago.)

Now, visit the Diversity link at the bottom of the Web page (**www.cotf.edu/ete/modules/msese/earthsysflr/species.html**). Have students answer the following questions:

- What is the most diverse group of living things? (Insects)
- Where are most land species found? (Most are found in tropical rainforests along the equator.)
- Why? (The region offers high rainfall, warm temperatures, and abundant energy.)

DAY 5 Recall the diversity of species from Day 4's activities. How does this diversity affect human environments? (Probe for answers—as you lead them to the need for goods and services for human survival.)

How many people are on Earth? Visit The U.S. Census clock at **www.census.gov/cgi-bin/ipc/popclockw**.

Visit David Levine's world clock at **www.ibiblio.org/lunarbin/worldpop** to compare today's figures with those of 1970.

Have students create a graph to visually show the world's population in 1970, 1980, 1990, and now. The graph should look something like Figure 12.

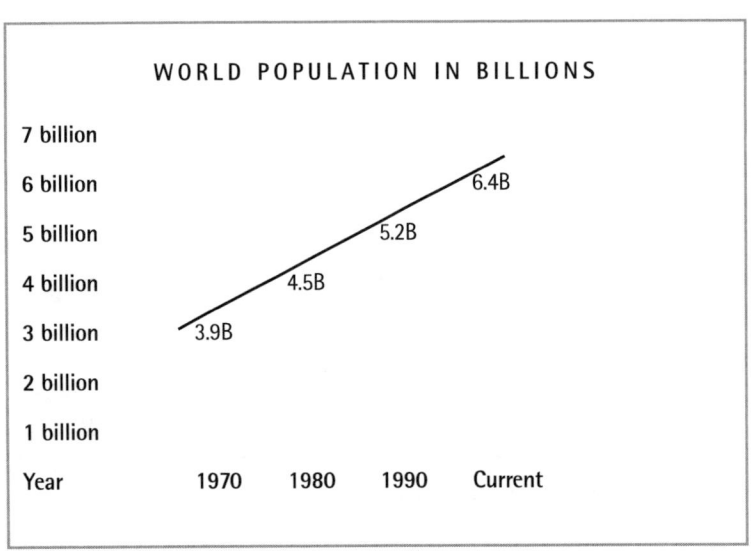

FIGURE 12. A graph depicting the world's population over time.

How does the increase in population affect resources? Who uses the most resources? Visit the Population Reference Bureau's site at **www.prb.org/Content/NavigationMenu/PRB/Educators/Human_Population/Environment4/Environment_Q_and_A1.htm** to discover statistics.

Have students create a graph to show the amount of resources the average person in India uses, compared with the amount of resources the average person in the U.S. uses (the factor is 30). The graph should look something like Figure 13.

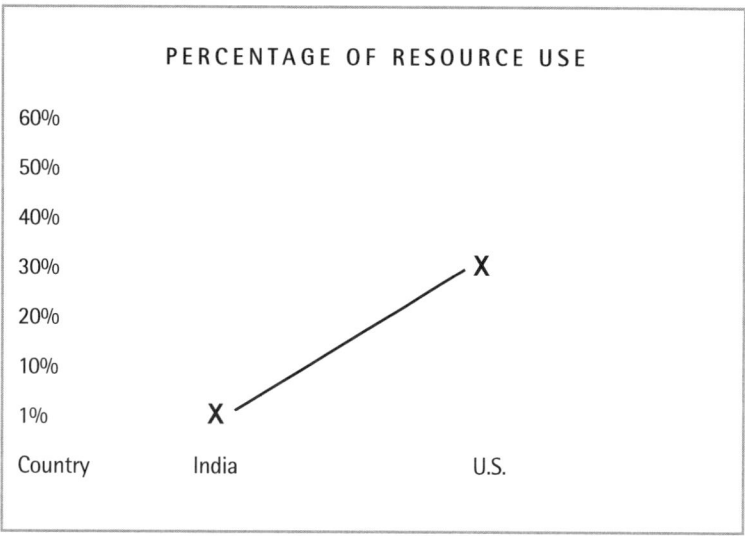

FIGURE 13. A graph comparing resources used by two countries.

What conclusions can be drawn about resource allocation and resource use?

DAY 6 Recall the resource allocation and population statistics from Day 5. How does this affect our world today?

Elicit student explanations of the words *export*, *import*, and *self-sufficient*. Ensure that they recognize that exports go out, imports come in, and self-sufficiency implies not needing either.

Visit the U.S. Census Bureau Foreign Trade Statistics at **www.census.gov/foreign-trade/www/**. Compare the trade data for 1989, 1997, and 2003.

Have students create a graph to visually display export and import levels for these years. The graph should look something like Figure 14.

What inferences can be drawn from these data?

DAYS 7–8 Have students work in groups to research one of the following countries, using the CIA World Factbook at **www.cia.gov/cia/publications/factbook/docs/profileguide.html** to discover the answers. After the answers are recorded on the Country Research Sheet, students should draw and color the country's flag. The U.S. facts are recorded on the Country Research Sheet for comparison purposes.

Have students select from the following countries (all these countries are along temperate zones): Azerbaijan, Belize, Bhutan, Borneo, Brazil, Ecuador, India, Iraq, Israel, Japan, Kenya, Sri Lanka.

SECTION 2—RESOURCE UNITS

FIGURE 14. A visual display such as this graph helps students draw inferences from the data they have collected.

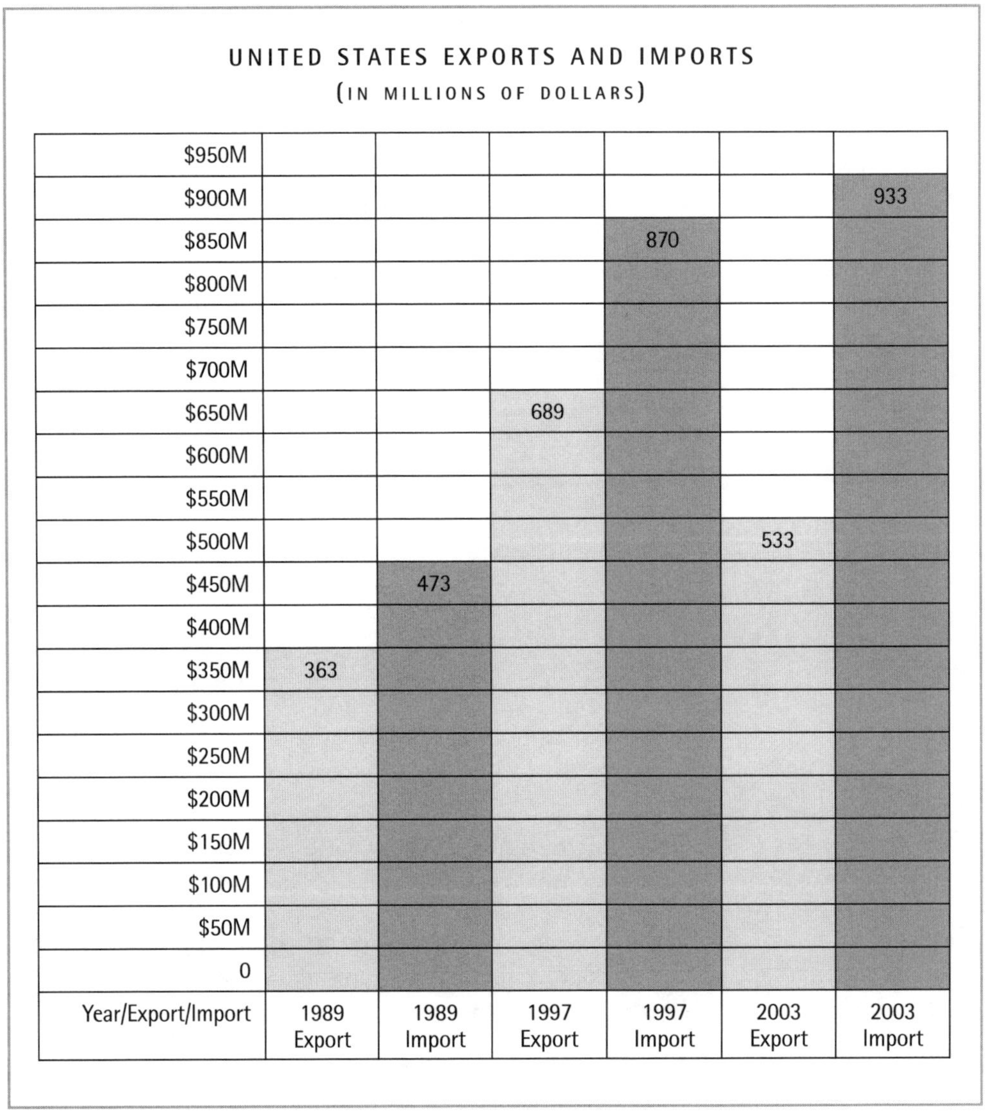

UNITED STATES EXPORTS AND IMPORTS
(IN MILLIONS OF DOLLARS)

Year/Export/Import	1989 Export	1989 Import	1997 Export	1997 Import	2003 Export	2003 Import
$950M						
$900M						933
$850M				870		
$800M						
$750M						
$700M						
$650M			689			
$600M						
$550M						
$500M					533	
$450M		473				
$400M						
$350M	363					
$300M						
$250M						
$200M						
$150M						
$100M						
$50M						
0						

DAYS 9–10 Have groups summarize the unit. Ask them to be sure to include the following information:

- From Day 2, tallies from the class interviews. What trends were noted?
- From Day 2, the five ecoregions discovered with descriptions of each.
- From Day 3, the definitions for the 12 vocabulary words (continent, volcano, mountain, plain and plateau, island, peninsula, cape, isthmus, valley, canyon, cliff, swamp).
- From Day 4, the chart on the world's ecoregions.
- From Day 5, the charts on population and resource use, as well as the inferences.
- From Day 6, the chart on imports and exports, with inferences.
- From Days 7 and 8, the chart on the assigned country.

Country Research Sheet

Directions: Using the CIA World Factbook at www.cia.gov/cia/publications/factbook/docs/profileguide.html, research one of the following countries: Azerbaijan, Belize, Bhutan, Borneo, Brazil, Ecuador, India, Iraq, Israel, Japan, Kenya, Sri Lanka. *(U.S. facts are provided here for comparison purposes.)*

Name of country	United States of America	
Continent	North America	
Latitude/longitude	38°00 N, 97°00 W	
Area comparative	½ size of Russia, ³/₁₀ size of Africa, ½ size of South America	
Coastline	19,924 KM	
Climate	mostly temperate, but also tropical, arctic, semiarid, and arid	
Terrain	mainly vast central plain, but also mountains, hills, broad river valleys, volcanic topography	
Natural resources	coal, copper, lead, molybdenum, phosphates, uranium, bauxite, gold, iron, mercury, nickel, potash, silver, tungsten, zinc, petroleum, natural gas, timber	
Environmental concerns	air pollution, acid rain, pesticide and fertilizer runoff, limited fresh water	
Geographic notes	world's third largest country by size	
Population	290 million	
Industries	leading industrial power in the world; highly diversified and technologically advanced; petroleum, steel, motor vehicles, aerospace, telecommunications, chemicals, electronics, food processing, consumer goods, lumber, mining	
Export commodities	capital goods, automobiles, industrial supplies and raw materials, consumer goods, agricultural products	
Import commodities	crude oil and refined petroleum products, machinery, automobiles, consumer goods, industrial raw materials, food and beverages	
Telephone main lines	194 million	
ISPs	7,000	
Internet users	165.75 million	
Airports	14,801	

SECTION 2—RESOURCE UNITS

Have students in groups analyze the information they have gathered. Ask them to prepare a five-paragraph essay detailing the three main ideas presented, the world's population, the distribution and allocation of resources, and biomes, and inferences the group has drawn from the analysis of this information.

DAY 11　Each group will present the information they found on their assigned country.

As a final exercise, have the students write six guided statements about where they live. Write these prompts on the board, and ask students to finish them.

I live in (city/state/country).

I live where telephone service to my dwelling (is/is not) available.

I live in the (Northern/Southern Hemisphere).

I live in a (desert/forest/coastal area/mountain zone).

I live at _____ feet above/below sea level.

I share my living space with _____ other humans.

Have students compare their answers with those of Day 1.

TEACHING TIPS　While teaching the unit, draw comparisons with the Galapagos Islands—nature's living experiment. Discuss how landforms enhance or inhibit trade routes, and the migration of people. Initiate discussions on why people have settled into your particular area. What made it valuable? What made it unique? Why would people wish to live there, instead of someplace else?

The Galapagos Islands are an example of "someplace else" where people might live. Traditionally the islands were isolated and simply a "stopping off" point, rather than a destination. This explains why the evolutionary processes occurred as they did. But here's where it gets tricky. Evolution is a word that evokes strong emotions, and students often associate it with religious beliefs. It is important that you emphasize that you are using this term and concept simply to mean "change that occurs over time," and it is not your intention to challenge any religious beliefs. Visit PBS's Evolution site for helpful information on discussing evolution in the classroom (**www.pbs.org/wgbh/evolution/library/faq/cat01.html#Q01**).

LESSON EXTENDERS　Ask students to visit the local chamber of commerce or tourism bureau to gather information about your particular area. What is highlighted? Nature? Commerce? Schools? What conclusions can be drawn about why people move to and stay in your area? Why did the area first become settled? Is the original reason (agriculture, trapping, commerce, etc.) still the reason people live there today?

Have students investigate the resources your area exports and imports. How has this affected the way your community has developed? For example, in downtown Glendale, Arizona, there is an abandoned red brick building built in the early 1900s to house sugar. It lies next to abandoned railroad tracks that once connected to the east/west transcontinental railroad routes. The city was built around these tracks.

With your students, look at the interstate routes that bisect your state. Why are they placed where they are? Do they mimic old trader's routes? Were they placed politically? Were they placed for military strategies? If the interstate highways were shut down, what would happen to your community? Draw conclusions about transportation, and how it affects us now.

UNIT 2: GALAPAGOS ARCHIPELAGO

DAY 1 Ask students what they know about Darwin. Ask where Darwin made his discoveries. Have them define an archipelago. Where is the Galapagos Archipelago? What other archipelagos can they name?

Using the CIA World Factbook, select Ecuador (**www.cia.gov/cia/publications/factbook/geos/ec.html**).

Direct students to examine the country's statistics. Have them pay particular attention to environmental issues, telephone lines and associated concerns, and the number of Internet users. Ask them to record this information.

During the next four days, groups of students will research the Galapagos Islands, learning the differences between endemic and introduced species, invasive species, species adaptation, human migration, and conservation efforts.

Have students begin their research with PBS's Destination: Galapagos Islands site (**www.pbs.org/safarchive/5_cool/galapagos/g21_history.html**). Ask them to record the definition of each linked word.

DAYS 2–3 Review key concepts. Where are the Galapagos Islands? What did Charles Darwin do on these islands? To which country do they belong? What is natural selection?

Have student groups read the PBS Galapagos information on geography and geology at **www.pbs.org/safarchive/5_cool/galapagos/g22_geo.html** and on weather at **www.pbs.org/safarchive/5_cool/galapagos/g24_weather.html**. Ask them to gather information on the linked terms and to take notes on their readings.

Students should then read the section on wildlife at **www.pbs.org/safarchive/5_cool/galapagos/g23_biology.html**. Students should take notes on which animals are endemic and which are a subspecies.

Have students read the information on natural selection at **www.pbs.org/safarchive/ 5_cool/galapagos/g48_glossary.html#more**. Ask them how natural selection applies to the Galapagos Islands. Students should analyze climate and geographic location to answer this question.

DAY 4 Groups will continue to research information on the Galapagos Islands. They will prepare a short report to present to their classmates, building upon the PBS site information. Students should pay particular attention to endemic species and problems with invasive species. How has the government of Ecuador chosen to handle these issues? What other ways could they be handled?

Have three groups of students review the following specific areas at Dr. Richard Rothman's Galapagos site (**www.rit.edu/~rhrsbi/GalapagosPages/Galapagos.html**).

- reptiles
- sea birds
- land birds

Ask another group of students to do research at Sea Cucumbers: Charles Darwin Foundation (**www.darwinfoundation.org/marine/FAQcuke.html**).

Another three groups of students can review the following areas at The Islands: Cornell University site (**www.geo.cornell.edu/geology/GalapagosWWW/ GalapagosMap.html**). Have them describe each island in their grouping and note peculiar facts about it.

- San Cristobal, Santa Fe, Santa Cruz, and Baltra
- Isabela, Fernandina, Santiago, and Espanola
- Marchena, Genovesa, Floreana, and Pinta

DAYS 5–6 In groups, students prepare a written report about their discoveries. They then will present their research findings. Their report will begin with the basic PBS information, and encompass what they have discovered in their groups. Groups will theorize how to protect the Galapagos Islands, specifically addressing endemic and introduced species, invasive species, species adaptation, human migration, and conservation efforts.

TEACHING TIPS Have students continue to look for and learn about endemic species. Why are they so different? Introduce the concept of adaptive radiation in species, and apply it to humans and their migration patterns.

Emphasize how the isolation of the islands has created their uniqueness, but also set them up for disaster. Everything that happens or is done there affects something else, and the results vary from compromised reproductive cycles to extinction. Mankind's footprint is most visible in this small environment.

While the theory of evolution has made these islands famous, the reality is that they are a microcosm of our world. Successful species have adapted, and continue to thrive. Yet the tourist industry, hailed as an economic boon to the islands, creates new and dangerous issues for the native flora and fauna as insects and critters sneak into luggage and are carried to the islands.

LESSON EXTENDERS

View the Construction Land Web site (**www.constructionlandonline.com**) with your students. It's designed for middle school grades, but the idea is to build a city while taking into account all the environmental and developmental parameters.

View the Cranford County Web-based simulation (**http://storm.simpson.edu/ ~proctorn/croatan/**) with your students. It's designed as a teaching tool, allowing participants to take actions and to see the resulting effects.

Consider garbage. Visit your local wastewater treatment plant for information. Visit a landfill. What is thrown away? How much garbage is generated annually per person? What happens to the garbage? Is it safer to burn it or bury it? Where is land available to bury garbage? Does it move into groundwater?

Research Love Canal in New York. Why is this site important to our lives today?

Assessment

CRITERIA	1 UNSATISFACTORY	2 SATISFACTORY	3 EXEMPLARY	SCORE
SOCIAL STUDIES STANDARDS				
Understanding of people, places, and environments	Understanding is not in evidence.	Student demonstrates acceptable understanding within the context of this project.	Student demonstrates exemplary understanding, making connections to personal experience through higher level applications of thinking.	
Understanding of interactions among individuals, groups, and institutions	Understanding is not in evidence.	Student demonstrates acceptable understanding within the context of this project.	Student demonstrates exemplary understanding, making connections to personal experience through higher level applications of thinking.	
Recognition of how people organize for the production, distribution, and consumption of goods and services	Understanding is not in evidence.	Student demonstrates acceptable understanding within the context of this project.	Student demonstrates exemplary understanding, making connections to personal experience through higher level applications of thinking.	
Recognition of global connections and interdependence	Understanding is not in evidence.	Student demonstrates acceptable understanding within the context of this project.	Student demonstrates exemplary understanding, making connections to personal experience through higher level applications of thinking.	
			Subtotal Points	

continued next page

Assessment

CRITERIA	1 UNSATISFACTORY	2 SATISFACTORY	3 EXEMPLARY	SCORE
NETS				
Understanding of social, ethical, and human issues related to technology	Understanding is not in evidence.	Student demonstrates acceptable understanding within the context of this project.	Student demonstrates exemplary understanding, making connections to personal experience through higher level applications of thinking.	
Use of technology research tools	Student lacks minimum proficiency in using these tools.	Student meets minimum proficiency for using these tools.	Student goes beyond minimum proficiency for using these tools, applying their use beyond the requirements of this project.	
Use of technology problem-solving and decision-making tools	Student lacks minimum proficiency in using these tools.	Student meets minimum proficiency for using these tools.	Student goes beyond minimum proficiency for using these tools, applying their use beyond the requirements of this project.	
TEAMWORK				
Team collaboration	Student doesn't work with team. Student doesn't try. Student produces no or little acceptable work.	Student works with others on team (regardless of individual likes or dislikes). Student consistently participates in team course work and satisfactorily completes all assignments.	Student facilitates group work—either as a consensus leader or consensus maker. Student positively encourages other teammates and is looked to for advice.	
Team assignments	Team doesn't work together. Team produces no or little acceptable work.	Team works together (regardless of individual likes or dislikes). Team satisfactorily completes all assignments in a timely fashion.	Team works well together, utilizing each member's strengths. All students are engaged and working beyond requirements.	
INDIVIDUAL WORK				
Individual assignments	Student doesn't complete all assignments. The completed assignments are unacceptable.	Student completes all assignments in a satisfactory and timely manner.	Student completes all assignments in a distinguished and intentional above-grade-level fashion. Assignments extend learning beyond the requirements and show evidence of synthesis of materials.	
Individual participation	Student does not participate in classroom assignments, or participation is disruptive, rather than constructive.	Student participates in classroom assignments in a satisfactory and constructive fashion.	Student participation is above satisfactory, and extends classroom learning for other students.	
			Subtotal Points	

continued next page

Assessment

CRITERIA	1 UNSATISFACTORY	2 SATISFACTORY	3 EXEMPLARY	SCORE
RESEARCH				
Research content	Topic is vague. No clear major points are presented. There is little or no evidence to support the points.	Topic is presented in an appropriate fashion. There is evidence to support the major points. Facts are correct.	Product surpasses the expectations. Information is synthesized in insightful ways. Facts are correct, and additional research is presented to elaborate.	
Research resources	Student uses few assigned resources. Analysis is inaccurate.	Student uses assigned resources and presents accurate analysis of same.	Student uses more resources than are assigned. Student finds and presents additional valid resources to complement and enhance subject.	
Research quality	Topic is scattered. Facts are inaccurate.	Topic is presented in a logical and clear fashion. Point "A" leads to Point "B," and so on. Writing is clear.	Topic is skillfully and thoroughly discussed and synthesized in an original way. Writing is fresh and distinguished.	
Research usage and mechanics	Several deviations from standard English usage are evident.	Minor deviations from standard English usage are evident.	No deviations from standard English usage are evident.	
OTHER CLASS WORK				
Understanding of the physical and human characteristics of places	Understanding is not in evidence.	Student demonstrates acceptable understanding within the context of this project.	Student demonstrates exemplary understanding, making connections to personal experience through higher level applications of thinking.	
Understanding of how human actions modify the physical environment	Understanding is not in evidence.	Student demonstrates acceptable understanding within the context of this project.	Student demonstrates exemplary understanding, making connections to personal experience through higher level applications of thinking.	
Recognition of how physical systems affect human systems	Understanding is not in evidence.	Student demonstrates acceptable understanding within the context of this project.	Student demonstrates exemplary understanding, making connections to personal experience through higher level applications of thinking.	
Understanding of the changes that occur in the meaning, use, distribution, and importance of resources	Understanding is not in evidence.	Student demonstrates acceptable understanding within the context of this project.	Student demonstrates exemplary understanding, making connections to personal experience through higher level applications of thinking.	
			Total Points	

The multicultural faces of America's teens.

Many Shades Are We: An Examination of the Diverse Cultures That Make Up America

DONNA ARCHIBALD

"Writers of color in America help validate American writing."

Russell Leong

UNIT OBJECTIVES

Student will be challenged to:

- Research the effect of various cultures within a major American city.
- Examine cultural diversity in the United States.
- Compare and contrast cultural diversity throughout the United States, noting patterns in ethnic concentrations.
- Examine factors that influence ethnic concentration patterns.
- Identify the effect of various cultures on business, the arts, education, and society.

SECTION 2—RESOURCE UNITS

SOCIAL STUDIES STANDARDS ADDRESSED

I   Culture
Social studies programs should include experiences that provide for the study of culture and cultural diversity.

III   People, Places, and Environment
Social studies programs should include experiences that provide for the study of people, places, and environments.

V   Individuals, Groups, and Institutions
Social studies programs should include experiences that provide for the study of interactions among individuals, groups, and institutions.

NETS•S ADDRESSED

2   Social, Ethical, and Human Issues
- Students understand the ethical, cultural, and societal issues related to technology.
- Students practice responsible use of technology systems, information, and software.

3   Technology Productivity Tools
- Students use technology tools to enhance learning, increase productivity, and promote creativity.

4   Technology Communications Tools
- Students use a variety of media and formats to communicate information and ideas effectively to multiple audiences.

5   Technology Research Tools
- Students use technology to locate, evaluate, and collect information from a variety of sources.
- Students use technology tools to process data and report results.

CENTRAL DISCIPLINE AREA

Cultural Diversity

The United States was built on the blending of many ethnic groups. These ethnic groups bring to the nation different languages, food, music, art, fashion, and traditions. As the U.S. continues to grow and change, the cultural composition of the major cities changes. The students will be challenged to study these changes and examine how these diverse cultures affect America as a whole.

UNIT DESCRIPTION

This unit is designed to be part of instruction about multicultural issues within social studies courses. After reading literature about different cultures, students will be placed into small groups and assigned a region of the U.S. Each group will pick a major city within that region to research for cultural diversity. They will explore the various cultures and report on the effect each culture has on:

- Business and economics
- The arts
- Education
- Society

Unit Tools

INTERDISCIPLINARY LINKS

Language Arts: Students will read nonfiction news stories that discuss cultural diversity within the United States. Students will draft a well-constructed final report reflecting on their research findings from both print and electronic sources. Students will illustrate their findings by placing a self-created graph within the report.

Mathematics: Students will collect data on the cultural diversity of a city. They will organize this information in spreadsheets and display it by using a graph. They will compare data from other class groups and compile a graph comparing their city to the nation as a whole.

Cultural Arts: Students will be exposed to a wealth of information about music, art, dance, and food through the study of cultures. The United States is rich with traditions, both new and old, that mold society. Students will be gathering artifacts reflecting the major city that they researched. They will share these artifacts with the class by using a multimedia application.

SPOTLIGHT ON TECHNOLOGY

Internet Research: The students will use the Web for research. Students must seek information on the cultural diversity within America's cities and report on their findings. They will learn effective searching techniques, the correct evaluation of Internet sites, and the proper format for citing Internet sources.

Spreadsheets: The students will use spreadsheet software to record and analyze data. They will create graphical representations of their findings.

Word Processing: Students will use word processing software tools such as grammar checkers, spelling checkers, margin adjusters, numbering and bullet features, and font formatting utilities to create a report that summarizes their findings.

Utility Tools: Students may choose to use a photo-editing tool such as Photoshop to edit scanned photos for insertion within their presentation.

Multimedia: The students will use a multimedia tool such as PowerPoint, iMovie, Pinnacle, or HyperStudio to create a presentation reflecting their learning. In the creation of their project, they will consider visual literacy concepts such as alignment, contrast, repetition, and placement of graphics.

SECTION 2—RESOURCE UNITS

TECHNOLOGY RESOURCES NEEDED

Hardware
computers with Internet access
video projector attached to a computer for presentations
scanner (optional)

Software
Web browsing software
word processing software
spreadsheet software
presentation software or multimedia software, such as PowerPoint, HyperStudio, iMovie, or Pinnacle
photo editing software (optional)

WEB AND LITERATURE RESOURCES

Web Resources
American Fact Finder:
 http://factfinder.census.gov/home/saff/main.html?_lang=en
Bucknell: Ethnic Groups and Immigration Statistics:
 www.isr.bucknell.edu/Collection_guides/Statistics/ethnic.asp
Center for Immigration Studies: **www.cis.org/index.cgi**
Changing America: **http://magma.nationalgeographic.com/ngm/data/2001/09/01/html/ft_20010901.3.html**
Changing America: Indicators of Social and Economic Well-Being by Race and Hispanic Origin: **http://w3.access.gpo.gov/eop/ca/index.html**
Council of Economic Advisors: Economic Report of the President (2003):
 http://w3.access.gpo.gov/eop/ca/index.html
Cultural and Human Geography:
 http://geography.about.com/cs/culturalgeography/
Demographic and Voting Statistics: **www.latinovote.com/popdata**
Digital History: **www.digitalhistory.uh.edu/database/subtitles.cfm?titleID=59**
Edsitement: Reference Shelf: **http://edsitement.neh.gov/reference_shelf.asp**
Education America Web Directory: **http://dirs.educationamerica.net**
Ethnic America Online: **www.ethnic-america.com/eaol/**
Information Resources on Ethnic Identity in the United States:
 www-sul.stanford.edu/depts/ssrg/adams/shortcu/ethi.html
MSN City Guides: **http://local.msn.com**
National Geographic's Xpeditions: **www.nationalgeographic.com/xpeditions/**
Newslink: Major Metro Newspapers: **http://newslink.org/daym.html**
Official City Sites: **www.officialcitysites.org**
United States Census Bureau: **www.census.gov**
United States Demographics: **www.tetrad.com/pcensus/usa/usadata.html**
United States Demographics by State: **www.marketingresources.org/Maps/United%20States%20Demographics%20by%20State.htm**
University of Cincinnati United States Cities Resources: **www.libraries.uc.edu/research/subject_resources/business/resource_city_us.htm**
Yahoo Get Local City Guides: **http://local.yahoo.com/u_s__states**

Literature Resources
The American Kaleidoscope, Lawrence Fuchs
Anthropology of an American Girl, H. T. Hamann

MANY SHADES ARE WE: AN EXAMINATION OF THE DIVERSE CULTURES THAT MAKE UP AMERICA

Culture Wars: Opposing Viewpoints, Mary E. Williams (Ed.)
Ethnic Chicago: A Multicultural Portrait, Peter d'A. Jones & Melvin Holli (Eds.)
Faded Mosaic: The Emergence of Post-Cultural America, Christopher Clausen
The Flag of Childhood, Naomi Nye
Guns, Germs, and Steel: The Fates of Human Societies, Jared Diamond
Hanging Together: Unity and Diversity in American Culture, John Hingham & Carl J. Guarneri
Heart of Darkness, Joseph Conrad
Islam and the West, Bernard Lewis
Minorities: A Changing Role in American Society (Information Plus Reference Series), John McCoy
Multiculturalism, Robert Emmett Long
Neighborhood Odes, Gary Soto
One-Time Dog Market and Other Hungarian Folktales, Irma Molar
Prejudice Across America: The Experience of a Teacher and His Students on a Nationwide Trek Toward Racial Understanding, James Waller
Privilege, Power, and Difference, Allan G. Johnson
Shopping for Identity: The Marketing of Ethnicity, Marilyn Halter
Words Under the Words, Naomi Nye
Writing Culture: The Poetics and Politics of Ethnography, James Clifford & George E. Marcus
Yellow: Race in America Beyond Black and White, Frank H. Wu
You Eat What You Are: People, Culture, and Food Traditions, Thelma Barer-Stein

PREPARATION

Assign students to read selections from various poetry and short story books, such as:

- Naomi Nye, *The Flag of Childhood*
- Naomi Nye, *Words Under the Words*
- Irma Molar, *One-Time Dog Market and Other Hungarian Folktales*
- Gary Soto, *Neighborhood Odes*

The teacher leads a discussion about the readings, highlighting the vocabulary used to describe the culture. Special attention should be paid to how the literature brings forth the flavor of the culture.

Have students look in the local phone book to:

- Find where ethnic restaurants are located in the community.
- Research the various businesses, noting if ethnic businesses are grouped in areas.

SECTION 2—RESOURCE UNITS

DAY 1 Begin the discussion of cultural diversity based on literature that has been read by the class. The discussion should include an exploration of the following questions:

- What is cultural diversity?
- What are some of the cultures found in the United States?

Relate the assigned readings to the cultural diversity in your local community. Guide the class discussion to explore any patterns found.

- Are there concentrations of various cultures within your city?
- What evidence did you discover to support your findings?
- How do the concentrations affect the businesses in the area?

After the discussion, put students in groups of no more than four. Explain the task that each group will do:

1. Each group will be assigned a region of the United States.
2. Each group will choose a major city within that region.
3. The group members will research that city to discover the following:
   - What is the percentage of each ethnic group within the city?
   - What effect do these ethnic groups have on business and other economic concerns, on schools, on the arts, and on society in general?
4. Students are required to gather facts, graphics, and music to create a multimedia presentation about the cultural diversity within that city.

Have each group start their research by going to Official City Sites at **www.officialcitysites.org**.

DAYS 2–6 Direct students to collect data and artifacts of the various cultures within the city they chose. You will act as a guide, listening, questioning, and clarifying the information each group finds. Have students start with the resources listed in this unit and then expand using effective searching techniques. You may want to review with the class information on scanning and saving pictures from the Internet. Using credible sources from the Internet and documenting them accurately is important, so you may also want to review the proper evaluation and citation of Internet sites. A good source for this is at EdSitement, **http://edsitement.neh.gov/reference_shelf.asp**.

DAYS 7–10 Each group needs to graphically represent the many cultures that make up their city. To do this, they need to place the data in a spreadsheet and create a pie graph, like the one in Figure 15.

Students will develop a multimedia presentation using PowerPoint, HyperStudio, iMovie, or Pinnacle. Teach or review the use of the selected multimedia software, emphasizing visual literacy skills. Some visual literacy concepts are:

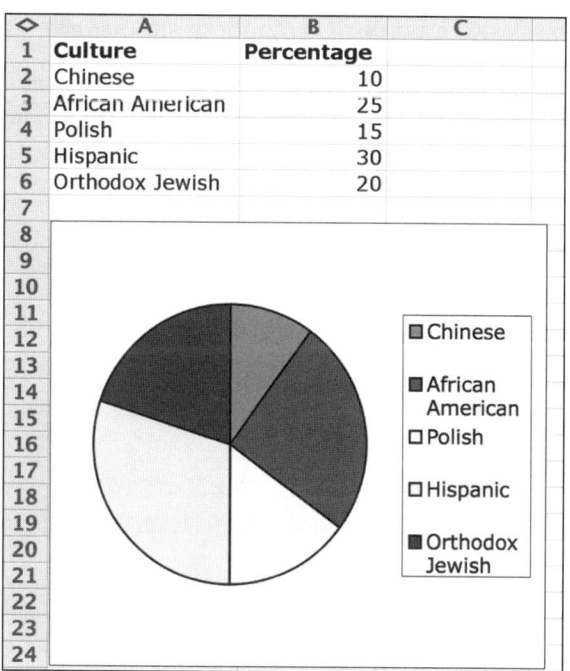

FIGURE 15. Example of a student-created spreadsheet and pie chart.

Alignment: Alignment refers to positioning elements so that they have a clear relationship to each other.

Lettering Styles: Allow the use of no more than two different type styles. These should harmonize with each other.

Contrast: Contrast adds emphasis. Students may add a bold contrasting text color to capture the viewer's attention.

Balance: Balance reference to the distribution of elements. The slide's elements should be placed so that the weight is equally distributed.

Rule of Thirds: Elements should be organized along any of the one-third dividing lines.

After discussing the use of the multimedia software, share with the groups the rubric you will use to grade the presentation. Have students use the remaining time to create their presentations. Move around to each group, making suggestions on design and content.

DAYS 11–12 Student groups will give their presentations, disclosing their findings. The information presented by each group should then be gathered and compiled in a national cultural diversity graph.

DAY 13 After watching all the presentations, lead a discussion on the commonalities and differences found in each city. Have each student use a word processor to compose a reflection paper that discusses the following:

SECTION 2—RESOURCE UNITS

- Compare your group's city with those of other groups. Were there patterns?
- Compare your city with the culminating graph of the nation.
- Provide a personal reflection on what you learned and how it changed your view of diversity.

TEACHING TIPS

The following suggestions are for organizing Internet resources:

- File bookmarks on your class browser before starting the unit.
- Use a Web-based bookmark organizer such as Backflip (**www.backflip.com**).
- Create a word processing document with the selected Internet sites and distribute it to students.
- Create a hotlist of resources that your school Webmaster can post on your class Web site for easy access from any location.

As students create their multimedia presentations, encourage them to view other group's presentations, making suggestions and general comments. By critiquing each other's projects, the students will learn from each other.

LESSON EXTENDERS

To extend the lesson, compile the findings on a multicultural map of the United States and discuss it with the class. Use the following steps as guideposts:

1. Create a large digital map of the United States. National Geographic's Xpeditions Web site (**www.nationalgeographic.com/xpeditions/**) offers a resource for digital maps.

2. Have each group place on the map digital pictures or other graphic elements representing the many cultural groups they found within their region.

3. When the map is completed and printed, display it in the room. Lead a discussion on any patterns of settlement that arise, or on particular concentrations of a certain ethnic group within a region. As a class, examine the factors that influence this behavior.

Another lesson extension idea is to post findings on the cultural diversity of the United States on a project Web site.

Author's note: A special thank you to Joyce Sevarino, Michael Kic, Cheryle Petrone, and Ann Penstone from Township High School District 214 for assisting me in gathering resources.

Assessment

CRITERIA	1 UNSATISFACTORY	2 SATISFACTORY	3 EXEMPLARY	SCORE
SOCIAL STUDIES STANDARDS				
Understanding of culture and cultural diversity	Understanding is not in evidence.	Student demonstrates acceptable understanding within the context of this project.	Student demonstrates exemplary understanding, making connections to personal experience through higher level applications of thinking.	
Understanding of people, places, and environments	Understanding is not in evidence.	Student demonstrates acceptable understanding within the context of this project.	Student demonstrates exemplary understanding, making connections to personal experience through higher level applications of thinking.	
Understanding of interactions among individuals, groups, and institutions	Understanding is not in evidence.	Student demonstrates acceptable understanding within the context of this project.	Student demonstrates exemplary understanding, making connections to personal experience through higher level applications of thinking.	
NETS				
Recognition of social, ethical, and human issues related to technology	Understanding is not in evidence.	Student demonstrates acceptable understanding within the context of this project.	Student demonstrates exemplary understanding, making connections to personal experience through higher level applications of thinking.	
Use of technology productivity tools	Student shows lack of minimum proficiency in using these tools.	Student meets minimum proficiency for using these tools.	Student goes beyond minimum proficiency for using these tools, applying their use beyond the requirements of this project.	
Use of technology communications tools	Student shows lack of minimum proficiency in using these tools.	Student meets minimum proficiency for using these tools.	Student goes beyond minimum proficiency for using these tools, applying their use beyond the requirements of this project.	
Use of technology research tools	Student shows lack of minimum proficiency in using these tools.	Student meets minimum proficiency for using these tools.	Student goes beyond minimum proficiency for using these tools, applying their use beyond the requirements of this project.	
			Subtotal Points	

continued next page

SECTION 2—RESOURCE UNITS

Assessment

CRITERIA	1 UNSATISFACTORY	2 SATISFACTORY	3 EXEMPLARY	SCORE
RESEARCH				
Research: print resources	Student used one resource.	Student used a selection of resources that included one from each: • Reference • Book • Journal	Student used a careful selection of resources that included one from each: • Reference • Book • Journal	
Research: electronic resources	Student did not make careful selections of electronic resources.	Student selected most of the electronic sources based on: • Authorship • Publisher • Bias • Accuracy • Currency	Student selected all electronic source based on: • Authorship • Publisher • Bias • Accuracy • Currency	
Research: documentation	Student did not provide citations.	Student provided correct citations for most of the sources based on American Psychological Association, Modern Language Association, or *Chicago Manual of Style* conventions.	Student provided correct citations for all sources based on American Psychological Association, Modern Language Association, or *Chicago Manual of Style* conventions.	
Research: gathering of resources	Student lost focus; therefore, information is not accurate and complete.	Student used a variety of resources, made careful selections, and revised the search when prompted.	Student used a variety of resources, made careful selections, and continually revised the search based on information found.	
GRAPH				
Graph data	Data are disorganized. Graph type is inappropriate, and labels are nonexistent.	Graph type fits the data. Data in tables have appropriate labels. Some disorganization is evident.	Graph type fits the data. Data in tables are well organized with appropriate labels.	
Graph labels	Several labels are missing.	One or two labels are missing.	All data are appropriately labeled.	
Graph format	Colors are muted and text is unclear.	Graph is relatively attractive. Colors clash or are in the same hue and do not complement each other. Text is clear.	Graph is well designed, using colors that go together or complement each other. Graph is easily read, the text is clear, and it is visually appealing.	
			Total Points	

The highest court in the United States.

From *Plessy* to *Brown:* Concept Mapping the U.S. Supreme Court

MATHEW MANWELLER

"It is emphatically the province and duty of the judicial department to say what the law is."

Justice John Marshall (Marbury v. Madison)

UNIT OBJECTIVES

Students will be challenged to:

- Research the development of American segregation case law from 1896 to 1954.
- Compare and contrast majority and dissenting opinions.
- Create a concept map illustrating the change in constitutional law between *Plessy* and *Brown*.
- Paraphrase and interpret historically significant case law.
- Role-play participants from the *Brown* case.

SOCIAL STUDIES STANDARDS ADDRESSED

I **Culture**
Social studies programs should include experiences that provide for the study of culture and cultural diversity.

II **Time, Continuity, and Change**
Social studies programs should include experiences that provide for the study of the ways human beings view themselves in and over time.

V **Individuals, Groups, and Institutions**
Social studies programs should include experiences that provide for the study of interactions among individuals, groups, and institutions.

VI **Power, Authority, and Governance**
Social studies programs should include experiences that provide for the study of how people create and change structures of power, authority, and governance.

X **Civic Ideals and Practices**
Social studies programs should include experiences that provide for the study of the ideals, principles, and practices of citizenship in a democratic republic.

NETS•S ADDRESSED

3 **Technology Productivity Tools**
- Students use technology tools to enhance learning, increase productivity, and promote creativity.
- Students use productivity tools to collaborate in constructing technology-enhanced models, preparing publications, and producing other creative works.

5 **Technology Research Tools**
- Students use technology to locate, evaluate, and collect information from a variety of sources.
- Students use technology tools to process data and report results.
- Students evaluate and select new information resources and technological innovations based on the appropriateness to specific tasks.

CENTRAL DISCIPLINE AREA

Constitutional Law

U.S. Supreme Court decisions take place every year, and they attract considerable attention from the public and students. Understanding important historical decisions sheds light on a nation's historical, cultural, and political development. Studying the desegregation cases that were handed down between 1896 and 1954 helps students understand the slow and incremental process of constitutional decision-making. Students will be challenged to understand how constitutional law is actually tied to the cultural norms of the time, and that as norms change, so does the law.

FROM *PLESSY* TO *BROWN*: CONCEPT MAPPING THE U.S. SUPREME COURT

UNIT DESCRIPTION

This unit explores how the Supreme Court evolves constitutional doctrine to accommodate current social and cultural values. Students will learn about the structural features of the court such as precedent, majority opinions, and dissenting opinions. They will be asked to read the landmark cases *Plessy v. Ferguson* and *Brown v. Board of Education,* critically interpreting the philosophies and reasoning behind the majority and dissenting opinions. Using online databases, they will research the intermediary cases that were issued between *Plessy* and *Brown,* examining the incremental nature in which the Court overturns established precedent. Students will use this research, in conjunction with concept mapping software, to create a concept map that illustrates how the dissenting opinion in *Plessy* eventually became the majority opinion in *Brown*. As a culminating project, students will research the actual arguments and participants associated with *Brown* and role-play the oral arguments of 1954.

Unit Tools

INTERDISCIPLINARY LINKS

History: It is important for students to understand the historical backdrop in which legal cases are decided. Students will have the opportunity to study the historical events surrounding the battle over desegregation in the United States and the eventual oral arguments before the Supreme Court.

Drama: Role-playing can be an effective pedagogical tool. Students who role-play historical events or participate in simulations tend to retain more of the information they learn. In this unit, students will conduct a recreation of the *Brown* case. Participants will become lawyers, justices, bailiffs, journalists, and courtroom observers.

SPOTLIGHT ON TECHNOLOGY

Word Processing: Word processing software is typically used for essays and other written assignments. This unit uses word processing software as a tool for taking notes, interpreting text, and paraphrasing legal language. Using the Track Changes feature in Word, students will insert their own thoughts, comments, and interpretations within the legal cases they are reading. Using Word in this manner will help students organize their thoughts without having to re-read the entire document. It also encourages students to put complicated legal language into their own words. (Use of the Track Changes feature is discussed in a sidebar in The Seven Pillars of the Constitution.)

Concept Mapping: Students will use concept mapping software to visually illustrate how constitutional decisions evolve over time. They will be challenged to create a concept map that highlights the majority and dissenting opinion for each major school desegregation case between 1896 and 1954. The concept map will eventually show how the dissenting opinion in *Plessy* became the majority opinion in *Brown*.

Internet Research: Students will use online legal databases to search for cases that dealt with school desegregation.

Instant Messaging (Optional): Students may use an instant messenger feature to participate in a synchronous communication activity.

TECHNOLOGY RESOURCES NEEDED

Hardware
computers with Internet access

Software
word processing software (with a Track Changes feature)
concept mapping software
Web browsing software
Timeliner software (optional)

WEB, LITERATURE, AND VIDEO RESOURCES

Web Resources
The Brown Quarterly: **http://brownvboard.org/brwnqurt/brwnqurt.htm**
Brown v. Board of Education Issue: Racial Segregation in Public Schools:
    www.pbs.org/jefferson/enlight/brown.htm
Brown v. Board of Education: The Case: **www.nps.gov/brvb/pages/thecase.htm**
Civil Rights: An Overview: **www.law.cornell.edu/topics/civil_rights.html**
Cornell Legal Information Institute:
    http://supct.law.cornell.edu:8080/supct/cases/topic.htm
Educational Attainment of Blacks Post Brown Vs. Board of Education: Has
    Primary and Secondary School Integration Made a Difference?:
    www.ncat.edu/~econdept/wp/cloud8a2002.pdf
FedLaw: **www.thecre.com/fedlaw/legal30.htm**
History of the Supreme Court:
    www.supremecourthistory.org/02_history/02.html
Interactive Constitution: **www.constitutioncenter.org/constitution/**
Introduction to the Court Opinion on the Brown v. Board of Education Case:
    http://usinfo.state.gov/usa/infousa/facts/democrac/36.htm
Introduction to the Court Opinion on the Plessy v. Ferguson Case:
    http://usinfo.state.gov/usa/infousa/facts/democrac/33.htm
Judicial Activism Reconsidered: **www.amatecon.com/etext/jar/jar.html**
Landmark Supreme Court Cases: Brown v. Board of Education:
    www.landmarkcases.org/brown/home.html
Landmark Supreme Court Cases: Plessy v. Ferguson:
    www.landmarkcases.org/plessy/home.html
Library of Congress (Brown materials):
    http://memory.loc.gov/learn/lessons/97/crow/crowhome.html
NARA Digital Classroom: **www.archives.gov/digital_classroom/lessons/
    brown_v_board_documents/brown_v_board.html**
New Evidence About Brown v. Board of Education: The Complex Effects of
    School Racial Composition on Achievement:
    http://ideas.repec.org/p/nbr/nberwo/8741.html
Plessy v. Ferguson Opinions:
    http://afroamhistory.about.com/library/blplessy_v_ferguson.htm
Supreme Court of the United States: **www.supremecourtus.gov**
Yale-New Haven Teachers Institute (teacher resources):
    www.yale.edu/ynhti/curriculum/units/1982/3/82.03.06.x.html

Literature Resources
    Brown v. Board of Education: A Civil Rights Milestone and Its Troubled Legacy, James T. Patterson
    The Color-Blind Constitution, Andrew Kull
    Constitutional Law: Individual Rights: Examples and Explanations (Examples & Explanations Series), Allan Ides & Christopher N. May
    Dismantling Desegregation: The Quiet Reversal of Brown v. Board of Education, Gary Orfield, Susan E. Eaton, & Elaine R. Jones
    Fifty-Eight Lonely Men, Jack Peltason
    From Brown to Bakke: The Supreme Court and School Integration, 1954–1978, J. Harvie Wilkinson
    Landmark Decisions of the United States Supreme Court I (Landmark Decisions Series), Maureen Harrison & Steve Gilbert (Eds.)
    On the Limits of the Law, Stephen Halpern
    Simple Justice: The History of Brown v. Board of Education and Black America's Struggle for Equality, Richard Kluger

Video Resources
    Eyes on the Prize (PBS Home Video)

teaching the unit

DAY 1   **Optional Anticipatory Set Activity**

Some teachers feel it is important for students to develop a solid understanding of racism and its effects upon people before studying the *Brown* case. Since all students in school today have never experienced a formal and governmentally enforced segregation system, the importance of *Brown* may be lost. One way to remedy the situation is to have students participate in a virtual society in which discrimination is based on some arbitrary criterion. For example, using instant messages in a local and controlled environment can be enlightening.

Have students select different colors for the text they will use in the instant messages. Then, randomly pick one color of text and have students discriminate against people who send messages using that color. Discrimination can take the form of ignored messages, responses that are curt and short, or even responses that are mildly critical. The instructor will need to set ground rules that everyone is comfortable with. The instructor may want to run the activity several times so that every student experiences the "virtual discrimination." It is important to debrief with a class discussion after the activity is complete so that students understand the rationale for the activity.

Students will need to be introduced to the concepts of precedent, majority opinions, and dissenting opinions. This can be done through a brief lecture or reading

SECTION 2—RESOURCE UNITS

assignment. To help students gain a firm understanding, teachers may want to have them read a recent case that contains both types of opinions and refers to earlier decisions. Almost any non-unanimous case will work. To save time, this part of the unit can be assigned as homework.

DAY 2   Students need to go online and find a copy of the decisions for *Plessy v. Ferguson* (1896) and *Brown v. Board of Education* (1954). Make sure they find both the majority and dissenting opinions (*Brown* was unanimous and has no dissent). For information, students can go to the Cornell Legal Information Institute at **http://supct.law.cornell.edu:8080/supct/cases/topic.htm**.

A simple search on Google will also work. Using the Cornell site will allow students to become familiar with searching within the database, a skill they will need later in the unit. If teachers are pressed for time, they may want to find the cases before class and provide students with the Web address.

After finding the cases, students should copy and paste them into a Word document. They should then save the file to their personal folder or to a disk they can keep.

DAY 3   Students need to read the decisions. However, while reading the decisions, they should make notes, add their own comments and opinions about the quality of the logic, and paraphrase important paragraphs using the Track Changes feature of Word. That way, when they go back to reexamine the documents later, their ideas will be color-coded and stand out within the passage. Students may also want to post questions within the document for later class discussions.

DAY 4   Once students have critically read both decisions, the instructor should lead a class discussion. The discussion should focus on some key topics, such as:

- How long did it take to get from *Plessy* to *Brown*?
- Why do you think it took so long?
- Why do you think the court eventually changed its mind?
- What is the relationship between the dissenting opinion in *Plessy* and the majority opinion in *Brown*?

The discussion should conclude with the teacher explaining the incremental nature of the evolution of constitutional law. The lecture should focus on the fact that the Supreme Court typically hands down several decisions, over time, which slowly change a doctrinal precedent.

DAYS 5-6   Students will go back to the online Cornell legal database. This time, they will be searching for other cases concerned with school desegregation between the time of *Plessy* and *Brown*. They can search by topic. The Cornell Legal Information Institute offers subsections on equal protection, race, segregation, and education. All of these topics have decisions that slowly rolled back the precedent of *Plessy*. As students find cases that are appropriate, they should cut and paste them into Word. As in Day 3, students should use the Track Changes feature to interpret the meanings of the decisions. They should be looking for the evolution of the Court's thoughts about the legality of segregation.

For students having trouble, here are the key cases they should be examining:

- *Cumming v. County Board of Education*
- *Gong Lum v. Rice*
- *Missouri ex rel. Gaines v. Canada*
- *Sipuel v. Oklahoma*
- *Sweatt v. Painter*
- *McLaurin v. Oklahoma State Regents*

As an optional requirement, students can use Timeliner to organize the cases chronologically.

DAYS 7-8 Based on the cases they have found online, students should create a concept map that illustrates the progression of cases from *Plessy* to *Brown*. In the concept map, each case should have a box that identifies the name of the case and a brief summary (one or two sentences) of the majority opinion. Where appropriate, a second box, with a summary of the dissenting opinion, should be linked to the majority opinion. This should be done for every relevant case the student studied. Next, students should link common ideas with lines and arrows. Within the links, students should explain the commonalities. A simple example is provided in Figure 16. However, actual concept maps should be much more inclusive and detailed.

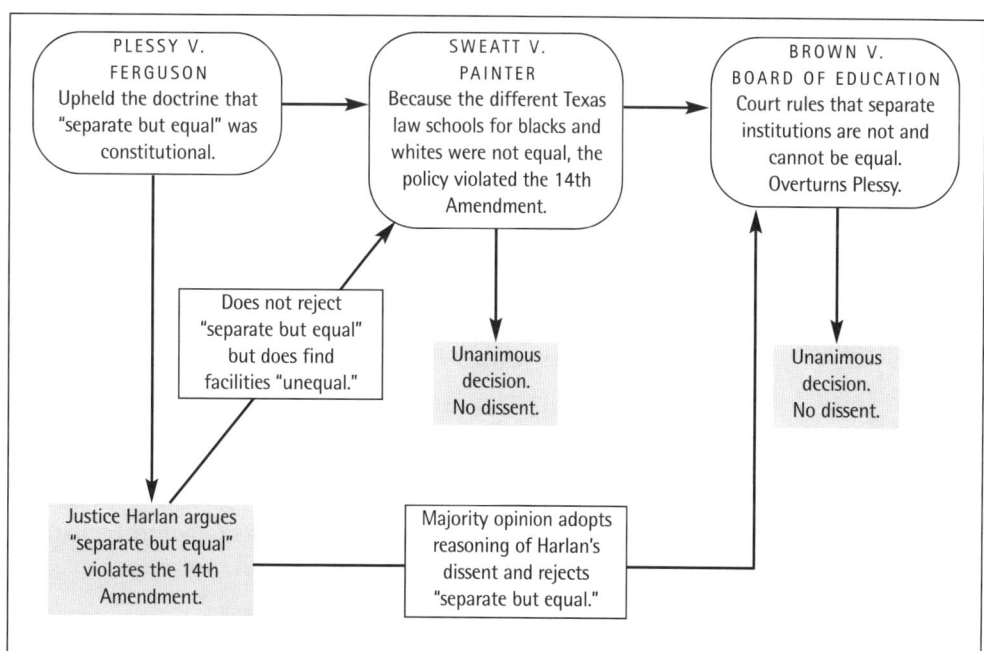

FIGURE 16. A concept map showing the progression of cases from *Plessy* to *Brown*.

SECTION 2—RESOURCE UNITS

DAYS 9–15 As a culminating activity, students should research the historical circumstances surrounding *Brown,* and organize a recreation. Research can take place on the Internet (the Web Resources section provides a good starting point) or in your school library. The teacher should assign roles: nine Supreme Court justices, two lawyers for Brown, two lawyers for the Topeka Board of Education, and one bailiff (to keep order and notify speakers when their time is up). The remainder of the students can be journalists or courtroom observers.

The complexity of the recreation is up to the teacher. However, at a minimum, lawyers should submit "briefs" to the justices before oral arguments (extra credit is a possibility here). This will allow justices to prepare questions for the lawyers during the oral arguments. Journalists and courtroom observers could be required to write newspaper articles and letters to the editor based on the proceedings. Justices could be required to write their own version of a *Brown* decision.

Consider videotaping the mock trial using a digital camera. You can use it as an example for future classes. Or, students may want to build Web sites about their projects. Digital video can easily be uploaded to the Web and used to enhance Web-based projects. And finally, you may want to show the video to the same class that produced the mock trial. Students may have new insights after they have had a chance to reflect on the project.

TEACHING TIPS Some Supreme Court decisions can be very lengthy. You may want to read the important decisions before assigning this project and then identify for your students the important passages they need to read or paraphrase. Oftentimes, online legal databases offer edited and truncated versions and an opinion. It may be easier for students to read the shorter versions.

In addition, it may be helpful for students to see a completed, or at least semi-completed, concept map before they begin. This will give them an idea of the expectations.

LESSON EXTENDERS Bring into class a local attorney from the community to lead a discussion on the effect, and limitations, of Supreme Court decisions.

Have students compare the *Brown* decision with the most recent affirmative action decisions such as *Bollinger* or even older cases such as *Bakke*. Have them write an essay examining the different interpretations of the Equal Protection Clause within the two cases.

Have students expand on their concept map to include cases that were affected or influenced by *Brown* but were not directly related to school desegregation. (Students would need to conduct searches on cases that cited *Brown*.)

Have students use semantic mapping software to create a flow chart indicating the process the courts follow in judging civil rights cases.

Students with advanced technology skills could record a digital video of the oral argument recreation and then upload it to a class Web site, or use it for the next open house.

Assessment

CRITERIA	1 UNSATISFACTORY	2 SATISFACTORY	3 EXEMPLARY	SCORE
SOCIAL STUDIES STANDARDS				
Understanding of culture and cultural diversity	Understanding is not in evidence.	Student demonstrates acceptable understanding within the context of this project.	Student demonstrates exemplary understanding, making connections to personal experience through higher level applications of thinking.	
Understanding of the ways human beings view themselves in and over time	Understanding is not in evidence.	Student demonstrates acceptable understanding within the context of this project.	Student demonstrates exemplary understanding, making connections to personal experience through higher level applications of thinking.	
Understanding of interactions among individuals, groups, and institutions	Understanding is not in evidence.	Student demonstrates acceptable understanding within the context of this project.	Student demonstrates exemplary understanding, making connections to personal experience through higher level applications of thinking.	
Recognition of how people create and change structures of power, authority, and governance	Understanding is not in evidence.	Student demonstrates acceptable understanding within the context of this project.	Student demonstrates exemplary understanding, making connections to personal experience through higher level applications of thinking.	
Understanding of the ideals, principles, and practices of citizenship in a democratic republic	Understanding is not in evidence.	Student demonstrates acceptable understanding within the context of this project.	Student demonstrates exemplary understanding, making connections to personal experience through higher level applications of thinking.	
			Subtotal Points	

continued next page

Assessment

CRITERIA	1 UNSATISFACTORY	2 SATISFACTORY	3 EXEMPLARY	SCORE
NETS				
Use of technology productivity tools	Student shows lack of minimum proficiency in using these tools.	Student meets minimum proficiency for using these tools.	Student goes beyond minimum proficiency for using these tools, applying their use beyond the requirements of this project.	
Use of technology research tools	Student shows lack of minimum proficiency in using these tools.	Student meets minimum proficiency for using these tools.	Student goes beyond minimum proficiency for using these tools, applying their use beyond the requirements of this project.	
CONCEPT MAP				
Number of cases cited	Two or fewer cases are cited in concept map.	Three to four cases are cited in concept map.	Five or more cases are cited in concept map.	
Use of dissenting opinions	No dissenting opinions are used in concept map.	One to two dissenting opinions are used in concept map.	Three or more dissenting opinions are used in concept map.	
Accuracy of paraphrasing decisions	Descriptions of most cases miss the main point of the decision, or students misstate the effect of the case.	Some descriptions miss the main point of the decision, or students misstate the effect of the case.	All cases are accurately paraphrased.	
Accuracy of links	Many links point to the wrong case, or students mistake the chronological order of the decisions.	A few links point to the wrong case, or students mistake the chronological order of the decisions.	All links accurately illustrate how precedent cases affect other cases.	
Organization and clarity	Concept map is disorganized and difficult to read.	Concept map is either disorganized and hard to follow, or is difficult to read.	Concept map is easy to read and easy to follow.	
Spelling and grammar	Project has many grammatical and spelling mistakes.	Project has a few grammatical and spelling mistakes.	Project has no grammatical or spelling mistakes.	
			Total Points	

Alexandra and Nicholas Romanov, Russia's last royal couple.

Prisoner's Dilemma: A Wireless Simulation of the Romanov Court

WALTER MCKENZIE

"The successful revolutionary is a statesman, the unsuccessful one a criminal."

Erich Fromm

UNIT OBJECTIVES

Students will be challenged to:

- Take on the avatar of a member of Czar Nicholas II's court in 1917.
- Interact using wireless handheld devices.
- Respond to text-based prompts.
- Make decisions based on prompts received.
- Form private alliances with other participants using wireless communication.
- Participate in the overthrow of the Czar.
- Debrief and discuss the simulation.

SOCIAL STUDIES STANDARDS ADDRESSED

IV **Individual Development and Identity**
Social studies programs should include experiences that provide for the study of individual development and identity.

V **Individuals, Groups, and Institutions**
Social studies programs should include experiences that provide for the study of interactions among individuals, groups, and institutions.

VIII **Science, Technology, and Society**
Social studies programs should include experiences that provide for the study of relationships among science, technology, and society.

X **Civic Ideals and Practices**
Social studies programs should include experiences that provide for the study of the ideals, principles, and practices of citizenship in a democratic republic.

NETS•S ADDRESSED

2 **Social, Ethical, and Human Issues**
- Students understand the ethical, cultural, and societal issues related to technology.
- Students practice responsible use of technology systems, information, and software.
- Students develop positive attitudes toward technology uses that support lifelong learning, collaboration, personal pursuits, and productivity.

3 **Technology Productivity Tools**
- Students use productivity tools to collaborate in constructing technology-enhanced models, preparing publications, and producing other creative works.

4 **Technology Communications Tools**
- Students use telecommunications to collaborate, publish, and interact with peers, experts, and other audiences.

6 **Technology Problem-Solving and Decision-Making Tools**
- Students use technology resources for solving problems and making informed decisions.
- Students employ technology in the development of strategies for solving problems in the real world.

CENTRAL DISCIPLINE AREA

Political Science

The prisoner's dilemma is a well-known scenario from game theory, and is a useful model for exploring the uncertainties and complications of political decision-making at a time of revolutionary change. At heart, the prisoner's dilemma is about anticipating how someone else—who may be an ally or an enemy—will act when given a choice between two options, and then choosing the option that will most likely further your own interests. For those who are not familiar with the prisoner's dilemma, here is a brief description.

Imagine two criminals arrested for a major crime they appear to have committed together. However, the police do not have sufficient proof to convict either one of anything more than a misdemeanor. So, the two prisoners are isolated from each other, and the police offer each a deal: the one who offers evidence against the other will be freed. If neither accepts the offer, they will be (in effect) cooperating against the police, and both will receive minimal punishment because of lack of proof. They both gain. However, if one of them betrays the other, the defector will gain more, since he is freed; the one who remained silent will receive the full punishment, since he did not help the police and there is now sufficient proof of a major crime. If both betray each other, both will be punished, but less severely because they have confessed and share the guilty plea. The dilemma arises from the fact that each prisoner has a choice between only two options—be loyal to and cooperate with his partner, or betray him—but cannot make a good decision without knowing what the other one will do. The dilemma is summarized in the table in Figure 17, with hypothetical "points" given to represent the different results.

FIGURE 17. The classic Prisoner's Dilemma.

OUTCOMES FOR PRISONER A		
	...and B cooperates	...and B betrays
If A cooperates...	+5, fairly good Both receive minimal punishment	-10, bad A receives full punishment B goes free
If A betrays...	+10, very good A goes free B receives full punishment	0, mediocre Both share lesser punishment

If we apply this dilemma to the political situation in a country that is ripe for revolution, we can see in Figure 18 that this set of outcomes tends to support the status quo. Two political groups or actors, faced with the choice of staying loyal to the crown or rebelling but unable to communicate openly with each other, must try to anticipate how the other group or actor will respond. The only way the revolution will be successful is if both groups "cooperate" and choose to rebel, but there is little incentive to cooperate. If we adapt the table in Figure 17 to this situation, we can see why in Figure 18.

FIGURE 18. The Prisoner's Dilemma as applied to the Romanov Court.

	OUTCOMES FOR ACTOR A	
	...and B rebels	...and B stays loyal
If A rebels...	+5 Successful revolution	−10 A is executed for treason
If A stays loyal...	+10, very good A is rewarded by the Crown for loyalty	0, mediocre Status quo

If A chooses to rebel and B does not, A may be executed; this is incentive not to rebel. If A stays loyal and B rebels, A will be rewarded; this is incentive to stay loyal. The safest choice for both actors, then, is to stay loyal if they don't know what the other is planning to do.

UNIT DESCRIPTION

Russia in 1917 was ripe for revolution, as poverty and civil unrest ripped apart the fabric of the nation. Losses during the First World War only contributed to the growing civil unrest among the common masses. Czar Nicholas II was aware of the political climate but continued to rule under the assumption that he remained a beloved figure among the populace. The difficulty for the royal family was knowing whom to trust in these turbulent times. This simulation places each student as a participant in the intrigue of the Russian court on the eve of revolution. It can serve as an excellent introduction to the rise of the Soviet Union or as a review study of Imperial Russia.

Unit Tools

INTERDISCIPLINARY LINKS

Language Arts: Students will receive and send text-based messages that will offer information on whom they can trust and with whom they can form alliances.

Mathematics: Students will use logic and deductive reasoning to try to maintain a political advantage throughout the simulation.

SPOTLIGHT ON TECHNOLOGY

Handheld Devices: Students will use information received through wireless communication to determine their action and reaction during the simulation.

TECHNOLOGY RESOURCES NEEDED

Hardware
 handheld wireless devices
Software
 handheld notepad application

PRISONER'S DILEMMA: A WIRELESS SIMULATION OF THE ROMANOV COURT

WEB AND LITERATURE RESOURCES

Web Resources

Clicking Anastasia: www.lostsecrets.com/education/edu.html

Emperor Nicholas II as I Knew Him: www.alexanderpalace.org/hanbury/

Glitter and Gloom: The Private and Public Conflict of the Last Imperial Family in Russia: www.honors.sbc.edu/HJSpr03/Hayes.htm

Last Days at Tsarskoe Selo: www.alexanderpalace.org/lastdays/

Letters From Tsar Nicholas to Tsaritsa Alexandra:
    www.alexanderpalace.org/letters/

Nicholas and Alexandra: www.nicholasandalexandra.com

Nicholas II: www.spartacus.schoolnet.co.uk/FWWtsar.htm

Russian History 1905–1930: www.dur.ac.uk/~dml0www/1905-30.html

Thirteen Years at the Russian Court: www.alexanderpalace.org/gilliard/

Literature Resources

The Fate of the Romanovs, Greg King

Last Tsar: The Life and Death of Nicholas II, Edvard Radzinsky

Rasputin: The Saint Who Sinned, Brian Moynahan

Shadow of the Winter Palace: Russia's Drift to Revolution, 1825–1917, Edward Crankshaw

What Became of Peter's Dream?: Courtculture in the Reign of Nicholas II, Anne C. Odom

White Crow: The Life and Times of the Grand Duke Nicholas Mikhailovich Romanov, 1859–1919, Jamie H. Cockfield

PREPARATION

Before beginning the unit, obtain a handheld computer for each student in your class. Have students draw the names below randomly to learn their identity, or avatar. On each handheld, have students type in the name, age, and occupation that will be their avatar for the duration of the project. (*Note:* Label each handheld so that you can be sure students will receive the same device each day.) Here are sample identities you may photocopy, cut into strips, and use:

Chaska Narbekov Age 56 Farmer	**Alexsandra Obukhovy** Age 20 Peasant	**Serge Charykovy** Age 16 Peasant	**Boris Dobrynin** Age 40 Noble
Lala Pavlovy Age 48 Noble	**Nicholas Romanov** Age 49 Czar	**Sonya Elchin** Age 36 File Clerk	**Ivan Federov** Age 19 Merchant
Alexandra Romanov Age 44 Czarina	**Mikhail Romanov** Age 39 Grand Duke	**Leo Gogol** Age 51 Noble	**Nadia Horvath** Age 22 Peasant

SECTION 2—RESOURCE UNITS

Obel Savenko Age 35 Farmer	**Radok Tikhan** Age 60 Noble	**Vlad Babinski** Age 17 Soldier	**Peter Bogdanov** Age 30 Farmer
Saltyk Ulminski Age 28 Cossack	**Holak Valentin** Age 19 Judge	**Igor Ikavits** Age 46 Farmer	**Jacob Junge** Age 33 Doctor
Zabor Wituski Age 53 Noble	**Bagram Wulff** Age 30 Peasant	**Alexei Karalov** Age 29 Soldier	**Leonid Khliebnikov** Age 24 Noble
Pater Zhakarov Age 27 Soldier	**Stanul Zubov** Age 55 Mayor	**Sleibor Lanskoi** Age 37 Lawyer	**Valentin Malechkin** Age 31 Noble
Mikhail Abirkov Age 25 Merchant	**Katrina Aleksiev** Age 49 Baker		

DAY 1 Establish the following ground rules for using the handhelds during this unit:

- You may communicate only by wireless; you cannot talk during the simulation each day.
- You must stay in the character of your avatar whenever communicating by wireless.
- You are not allowed to tell your occupation during the simulation.
- Once you send out a message you must wait for a response before you send a second message or response.
- You are not to discuss your avatar outside of class until the unit is over.
- If you are not sure what to do, send your question to the teacher using the wireless device.

Have students use Web-based and text resources to study the lives of their avatars during the reign of Nicholas II.

Ask each student to consider their perception of the Czar in the role of the avatar they have been assigned and write a quick summary of their thoughts in the handheld notepad.

DAY 2 Distribute handhelds and ask students to communicate with one another using their wireless devices, sharing their views of Russia in 1917. There should be no oral discussion; students will know who they are communicating with only by the avatars they meet using their handheld.

DAY 3 Ask students to list in their notepad which avatars they perceive themselves to have the most in common with, based on their Day 2 interaction. Emphasize that this is a dangerous time in Russia, and no one openly declares his or her support of or opposition to the Czar.

Ask students to continue to interact with one another, feeling each other out as to their political views.

DAY 4 Have students identify the names of avatars they perceive to be possible allies in their notepad.

Ask students to continue to interact with one another, giving clues about their avatar's occupation and political views.

At the end of the period have students make a notepad list of the names of avatars they perceive as being potential political adversaries.

DAY 5 Distribute the handhelds and send out this message to the entire class using your wireless device:

> "They are plotting to arrest the Czar and create a provisional government. All those who love mother Russia must choose their destiny!"

Allow time for students to express their reaction to this news with their perceived allies.

In the notepad, ask students to share what they plan to do if the Czar is actually arrested.

DAY 6 Distribute the handhelds and send out a message to the soldiers to arrest anyone they perceive as a traitor to the Czar.

Allow time for the soldiers to send out messages to those avatars they wish to arrest.

At the end of the session ask those avatars who were notified of their arrest to please stand and move to an isolated corner of the room. Advise them to return to the same corner at the beginning of the next class. Arrested avatars can still communicate wirelessly, but they can no longer be allowed to help the Czar or his enemies.

DAY 7 Distribute handhelds and send out the following wireless message:

> "A Cossack has broken through palace security and attempted to assassinate the Czar! If he is identified he will be shot on sight! Please help us find this rogue traitor!"

Allow students time to try to determine which avatar is the Cossack.

At the end of class have each student send you a wireless message of which avatar they believe is the Cossack.

DAY 8 Distribute handhelds and send out an announcement concerning the number of students who identified the Cossack correctly. Include the following information:

"The Cossack is still on the loose. If he is caught hiding among you, you too will be shot as a traitor! Be a patriot and turn him in!"

Tell students that by the end of the class they will be asked to stand and verbally identify the Cossack. If they are correct they will be heroes. If they are incorrect they will be jailed.

Send students with incorrect answers to the corner where other arrested avatars already reside.

DAY 9 Distribute handhelds and send out an announcement that the Czar has left the palace and is in hiding among the common people. Include the following message:

"The revolutionary council will reward any citizen who can identify the Czar and bring him to justice with a cash reward!"

Allow students time to communicate and try to determine who among them is the Czar. Students may opt to confuse other avatars to help protect the Czar, or to help offer clues of who they believe the Czar actually is.

At the end of the class ask each student to send the teacher a wireless message indicating who they believe to be the Czar.

DAY 10 Distribute handhelds and send out an announcement that the Czar has been arrested. Advise everyone to find allies whom they can trust during this uncertain political time.

Ask students to make a notepad list of which avatars they believe to be their allies.

Bring the class back together and have an oral discussion in which students:

- One at a time stand and reveal their avatar
- Reveal their avatar's true political alliance
- Share the list of avatars they believe to be allies

Discuss the experience of trying to be politically safe while operating in a dangerous environment. Consider what the consequences would have actually been in 1917 Russia if they did not trust the right people. Transfer these implications to other historical events you have studied.

TEACHING TIPS Be sure to consistently enforce the rules for participating in the simulation.

Remember to charge the handheld computers nightly.

Make sure students save their work each day before shutting down their handhelds.

LESSON EXTENDERS

Have students write an account of their experience as the avatar in the simulation. Ask them to tie in their experience with actual facts about the overthrow of Nicholas II.

Create a Web site that showcases each avatar and shares his or her perceptions about the political climate and alliances on which they rely.

Use student skills with handheld wireless devices to complete additional simulations during the school year.

Assessment

CRITERIA	1 UNSATISFACTORY	2 SATISFACTORY	3 EXEMPLARY	SCORE
SOCIAL STUDIES STANDARDS				
Understanding of individual development and identity	Understanding is not in evidence.	Student demonstrates acceptable understanding within the context of this project.	Student demonstrates exemplary understanding, making connections to personal experience through higher level applications of thinking.	
Understanding of interactions among individuals, groups, and institutions	Understanding is not in evidence.	Student demonstrates acceptable understanding within the context of this project.	Student demonstrates exemplary understanding, making connections to personal experience through higher level applications of thinking.	
Recognition of relationships among science, technology, and society	Understanding is not in evidence.	Student demonstrates acceptable understanding within the context of this project.	Student demonstrates exemplary understanding, making connections to personal experience through higher level applications of thinking.	
Understanding of the ideals, principles, and practices of citizenship in a democratic republic	Understanding is not in evidence.	Student demonstrates acceptable understanding within the context of this project.	Student demonstrates exemplary understanding, making connections to personal experience through higher level applications of thinking.	
			Subtotal Points	

continued next page

SECTION 2—RESOURCE UNITS

Assessment

CRITERIA	1 UNSATISFACTORY	2 SATISFACTORY	3 EXEMPLARY	SCORE
NETS				
Recognition of social, ethical, and human issues related to technology	Understanding is not in evidence.	Student demonstrates acceptable understanding within the context of this project.	Student demonstrates exemplary understanding, making connections to personal experience through higher level applications of thinking.	
Use of technology productivity tools	Student shows lack of minimum proficiency in using these tools.	Student meets minimum proficiency for using these tools.	Student goes beyond minimum proficiency for using these tools, applying their use beyond the requirements of this project.	
Use of technology communications tools	Student shows lack of minimum proficiency in using these tools.	Student meets minimum proficiency for using these tools.	Student goes beyond minimum proficiency for using these tools, applying their use beyond the requirements of this project.	
Use of technology problem-solving and decision-making tools	Student shows lack of minimum proficiency in using these tools.	Student meets minimum proficiency for using these tools.	Student goes beyond minimum proficiency for using these tools, applying their use beyond the requirements of this project.	
SIMULATION				
Following simulation rules	Student could not follow the rules of the simulation.	Student communicated using wireless technology with only occasional lapses in following the rules.	Student consistently followed the rules of the simulation.	
Staying in character	Student could not stay in character consistently.	Student stayed in character most of the time.	Student stayed in character consistently.	
Collaboration and participation	Student did not contribute to the simulation.	Student contributed to the simulation as required.	Student contributed to the simulation actively.	
Political reasoning	Student did not determine allies and enemies with any accuracy.	Student determined allies and enemies with some accuracy.	Student determined allies and enemies with a high degree of accuracy.	
			Total Points	

appendix

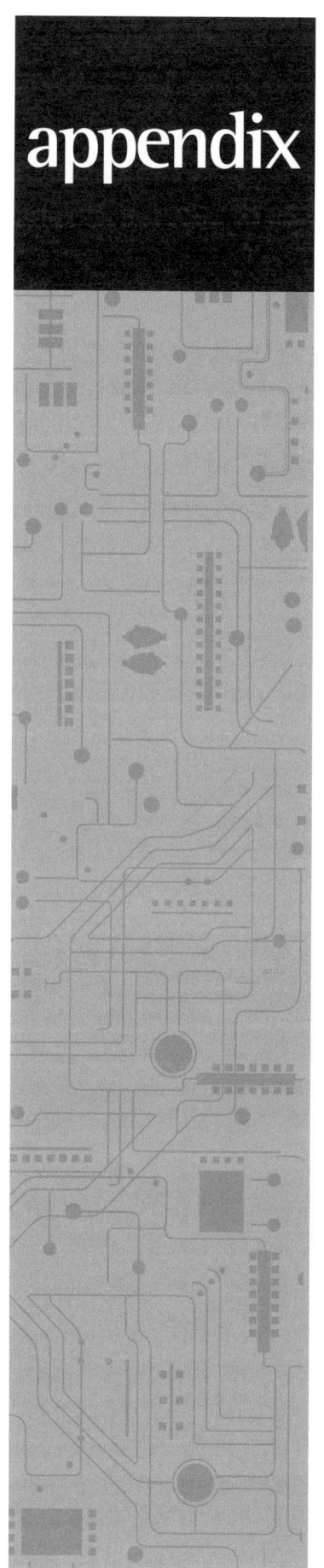

NATIONAL EDUCATIONAL TECHNOLOGY STANDARDS FOR STUDENTS (NETS•S)

NATIONAL EDUCATIONAL TECHNOLOGY STANDARDS FOR TEACHERS (NETS•T)

NATIONAL EDUCATIONAL TECHNOLOGY STANDARDS FOR ADMINISTRATORS (NETS•A)

SOCIAL STUDIES STANDARDS

APPENDIX

National Educational Technology Standards for Students (NETS•S)

The National Educational Technology Standards for Students are divided into six broad categories. Standards within each category are to be introduced, reinforced, and mastered by students. Teachers can use these standards as guidelines for planning technology-based activities in which students achieve success in learning, communication, and life skills.

1. **Basic Operations and Concepts**
   - Students demonstrate a sound understanding of the nature and operation of technology systems.
   - Students are proficient in the use of technology.

2. **Social, Ethical, and Human Issues**
   - Students understand the ethical, cultural, and societal issues related to technology.
   - Students practice responsible use of technology systems, information, and software.
   - Students develop positive attitudes toward technology uses that support lifelong learning, collaboration, personal pursuits, and productivity.

3. **Technology Productivity Tools**
   - Students use technology tools to enhance learning, increase productivity, and promote creativity.
   - Students use productivity tools to collaborate in constructing technology-enhanced models, preparing publications, and producing other creative works.

4. **Technology Communications Tools**
   - Students use telecommunications to collaborate, publish, and interact with peers, experts, and other audiences.
   - Students use a variety of media and formats to communicate information and ideas effectively to multiple audiences.

5. **Technology Research Tools**
   - Students use technology to locate, evaluate, and collect information from a variety of sources.
   - Students use technology tools to process data and report results.
   - Students evaluate and select new information resources and technological innovations based on the appropriateness to specific tasks.

6. **Technology Problem-Solving and Decision-Making Tools**
   - Students use technology resources for solving problems and making informed decisions.
   - Students employ technology in the development of strategies for solving problems in the real world.

APPENDIX

National Educational Technology Standards for Teachers (NETS•T)

All classroom teachers should be prepared to meet the following standards and performance indicators.

I Technology Operations and Concepts

Teachers demonstrate a sound understanding of technology operations and concepts. Teachers:

- A. demonstrate introductory knowledge, skills, and understanding of concepts related to technology (as described in the ISTE National Educational Technology Standards for Students).
- B. demonstrate continual growth in technology knowledge and skills to stay abreast of current and emerging technologies.

II Planning and Designing Learning Environments and Experiences

Teachers plan and design effective learning environments and experiences supported by technology. Teachers:

- A. design developmentally appropriate learning opportunities that apply technology-enhanced instructional strategies to support the diverse needs of learners.
- B. apply current research on teaching and learning with technology when planning learning environments and experiences.
- C. identify and locate technology resources and evaluate them for accuracy and suitability.
- D. plan for the management of technology resources within the context of learning activities.
- E. plan strategies to manage student learning in a technology-enhanced environment.

III Teaching, Learning, and the Curriculum

Teachers implement curriculum plans that include methods and strategies for applying technology to maximize student learning. Teachers:

- A. facilitate technology-enhanced experiences that address content standards and student technology standards.
- B. use technology to support learner-centered strategies that address the diverse needs of students.
- C. apply technology to develop students' higher order skills and creativity.
- D. manage student learning activities in a technology-enhanced environment.

IV Assessment and Evaluation

Teachers apply technology to facilitate a variety of effective assessment and evaluation strategies. Teachers:

- A. apply technology in assessing student learning of subject matter using a variety of assessment techniques.
- B. use technology resources to collect and analyze data, interpret results, and communicate findings to improve instructional practice and maximize student learning.
- C. apply multiple methods of evaluation to determine students' appropriate use of technology resources for learning, communication, and productivity.

APPENDIX

V Productivity and Professional Practice

Teachers use technology to enhance their productivity and professional practice. Teachers:

- A. use technology resources to engage in ongoing professional development and lifelong learning.
- B. continually evaluate and reflect on professional practice to make informed decisions regarding the use of technology in support of student learning.
- C. apply technology to increase productivity.
- D. use technology to communicate and collaborate with peers, parents, and the larger community in order to nurture student learning.

VI Social, Ethical, Legal, and Human Issues

Teachers understand the social, ethical, legal, and human issues surrounding the use of technology in PK–12 schools and apply that understanding in practice. Teachers:

- A. model and teach legal and ethical practice related to technology use.
- B. apply technology resources to enable and empower learners with diverse backgrounds, characteristics, and abilities.
- C. identify and use technology resources that affirm diversity.
- D. promote safe and healthy use of technology resources.
- E. facilitate equitable access to technology resources for all students.

APPENDIX

National Educational Technology Standards for Administrators (NETS•A)

All school administrators should be prepared to meet the following standards and performance indicators. These standards are a national consensus among educational stakeholders regarding what best indicates effective school leadership for comprehensive and appropriate use of technology in schools.

I Leadership and Vision

Educational leaders inspire a shared vision for comprehensive integration of technology and foster an environment and culture conducive to the realization of that vision. Educational leaders:

A. facilitate the shared development by all stakeholders of a vision for technology use and widely communicate that vision.
B. maintain an inclusive and cohesive process to develop, implement, and monitor a dynamic, long-range, and systemic technology plan to achieve the vision.
C. foster and nurture a culture of responsible risk-taking and advocate policies promoting continuous innovation with technology.
D. use data in making leadership decisions.
E. advocate for research-based effective practices in use of technology.
F. advocate, on the state and national levels, for policies, programs, and funding opportunities that support implementation of the district technology plan.

II Learning and Teaching

Educational leaders ensure that curricular design, instructional strategies, and learning environments integrate appropriate technologies to maximize learning and teaching. Educational leaders:

A. identify, use, evaluate, and promote appropriate technologies to enhance and support instruction and standards-based curriculum leading to high levels of student achievement.
B. facilitate and support collaborative technology-enriched learning environments conducive to innovation for improved learning.
C. provide for learner-centered environments that use technology to meet the individual and diverse needs of learners.
D. facilitate the use of technologies to support and enhance instructional methods that develop higher-level thinking, decision-making, and problem-solving skills.
E. provide for and ensure that faculty and staff take advantage of quality professional learning opportunities for improved learning and teaching with technology.

III Productivity and Professional Practice

Educational leaders apply technology to enhance their professional practice and to increase their own productivity and that of others. Educational leaders:

A. model the routine, intentional, and effective use of technology.
B. employ technology for communication and collaboration among colleagues, staff, parents, students, and the larger community.

C. create and participate in learning communities that stimulate, nurture, and support faculty and staff in using technology for improved productivity.
D. engage in sustained, job-related professional learning using technology resources.
E. maintain awareness of emerging technologies and their potential uses in education.
F. use technology to advance organizational improvement.

IV Support, Management, and Operations

Educational leaders ensure the integration of technology to support productive systems for learning and administration. Educational leaders:

A. develop, implement, and monitor policies and guidelines to ensure compatibility of technologies.
B. implement and use integrated technology-based management and operations systems.
C. allocate financial and human resources to ensure complete and sustained implementation of the technology plan.
D. integrate strategic plans, technology plans, and other improvement plans and policies to align efforts and leverage resources.
E. implement procedures to drive continuous improvements of technology systems and to support technology replacement cycles.

V Assessment and Evaluation

Educational leaders use technology to plan and implement comprehensive systems of effective assessment and evaluation. Educational leaders:

A. use multiple methods to assess and evaluate appropriate uses of technology resources for learning, communication, and productivity.
B. use technology to collect and analyze data, interpret results, and communicate findings to improve instructional practice and student learning.
C. assess staff knowledge, skills, and performance in using technology and use results to facilitate quality professional development and to inform personnel decisions.
D. use technology to assess, evaluate, and manage administrative and operational systems.

VI Social, Legal, and Ethical Issues

Educational leaders understand the social, legal, and ethical issues related to technology and model responsible decision-making related to these issues. Educational leaders:

A. ensure equity of access to technology resources that enable and empower all learners and educators.
B. identify, communicate, model, and enforce social, legal, and ethical practices to promote responsible use of technology.
C. promote and enforce privacy, security, and online safety related to the use of technology.
D. promote and enforce environmentally safe and healthy practices in the use of technology.
E. participate in the development of policies that clearly enforce copyright law and assign ownership of intellectual property developed with district resources.

This material was originally produced as a project of the Technology Standards for School Administrators Collaborative.

APPENDIX

Social Studies Standards

Performance Expectations for High School

I   Culture

Social studies programs should include experiences that provide for the study of culture and cultural diversity, so that the learner can:

   a. analyze and explain the ways groups, societies, and cultures address human needs and concerns;
   b. predict how data and experiences may be interpreted by people from diverse cultural perspectives and frames of reference;
   c. apply an understanding of culture as an integrated whole that explains the functions and interactions of language, literature, the arts, traditions, beliefs and values, and behavior patterns;
   d. compare and analyze societal patterns for preserving and transmitting culture while adapting to environmental or social change;
   e. demonstrate the value of cultural diversity, as well as cohesion, within and across groups;
   f. interpret patterns of behavior reflecting values and attitudes that contribute or pose obstacles to cross-cultural understanding;
   g. construct reasoned judgments about specific cultural responses to persistent human issues;
   h. explain and apply ideas, theories, and modes of inquiry drawn from anthropology and sociology in the examination of persistent issues and social problems.

II   Time, Continuity, and Change

Social studies programs should include experiences that provide for the study of the ways human beings view themselves in and over time, so that the learner can:

   a. demonstrate that historical knowledge and the concept of time are socially influenced constructions that lead historians to be selective in the questions they seek to answer and the evidence they use;
   b. apply key concepts such as time, chronology, causality, change, conflict, and complexity to explain, analyze, and show connections among patterns of historical change and continuity;
   c. identify and describe significant historical periods and patterns of change within and across cultures, such as the development of ancient cultures and civilizations, the rise of nation-states, and social, economic, and political revolutions;
   d. systematically employ processes of critical historical inquiry to reconstruct and reinterpret the past, such as using a variety of sources and checking their credibility, validating and weighing evidence for claims, and searching for causality;
   e. investigate, interpret, and analyze multiple historical and contemporary viewpoints within and across cultures related to important events, recurring dilemmas, and persistent issues, while employing empathy, skepticism, and critical judgement;
   f. apply ideas, theories, and modes of historical inquiry to analyze historical and contemporary developments, and to inform and evaluate actions concerning public policy issues.

APPENDIX

III People, Places, and Environments

Social studies programs should include experiences that provide for the study of people, places, and environments, so that the learner can:

   a. refine mental maps of locales, regions, and the world that demonstrate understanding of relative location, direction, size, and shape;
   b. create, interpret, use, and synthesize information from various representations of the earth, such as maps, globes, and photographs;
   c. use appropriate resources, data sources, and geographic tools such as aerial photographs, satellite images, geographic information systems (GIS), map projections, and cartography to generate, manipulate, and interpret information such as atlases, data bases, grid systems, charts, graphs, and maps;
   d. calculate distance, scale, area, and density, and distinguish spatial distribution patterns;
   e. describe, differentiate, and explain the relationships among various regional and global patterns of geographic phenomena such as landforms, soils, climate, vegetation, natural resources, and population;
   f. use knowledge of physical system changes such as seasons, climate and weather, and the water cycle to explain geographic phenomena;
   g. describe and compare how people create places that reflect culture, human needs, government policy, and current values and ideals as they design and build specialized buildings, neighborhoods, shopping centers, urban centers, industrial parks, and the like;
   h. examine, interpret, and analyze physical and cultural patterns and their interactions, such as land use, settlement patterns, cultural transmission of customs and ideas, and ecosystem changes;
   i. describe and assess ways that historical events have been influenced by, and have influenced, physical and human geographic factors in local, regional, national, and global settings;
   j. analyze and evaluate social and economic effects of environmental changes and crises resulting from phenomena such as floods, storms, and drought;
   k. propose, compare, and evaluate alternative policies for the use of land and other resources in communities, regions, nations, and the world.

IV Individual Development and Identity

Social studies programs should include experiences that provide for the study of individual development and identity, so that the learner can:

   a. articulate personal connections to time, place, and social/cultural systems;
   b. identify, describe, and express appreciation for the influences of various historical and contemporary cultures on an individual's daily life;
   c. describe the ways family, religion, gender, ethnicity, nationality, socioeconomic status, and other group and cultural influences contribute to the development of a sense of self;
   d. apply concepts, methods, and theories about the study of human growth and development, such as physical endowment, learning, motivation, behavior, perception, and personality;
   e. examine the interactions of ethnic, national, or cultural influences in specific situations or events;
   f. analyze the role of perceptions, attitudes, values, and beliefs in the development of personal identity;
   g. compare and evaluate the impact of stereotyping, conformity, acts of altruism, and other behaviors on individuals and groups;
   h. work independently and cooperatively within groups and institutions to accomplish goals;
   i. examine factors that contribute to and damage one's mental health and analyze issues related to mental health and behavioral disorders in contemporary society.

V Individuals, Groups, and Institutions

Social studies programs should include experiences that provide for the study of interactions among individuals, groups, and institutions, so that the learner can:

a. apply concepts such as role, status, and social class in describing the connections and interactions of individuals, groups, and institutions in society;
b. analyze group and institutional influences on people, events, and elements of culture in both historical and contemporary settings;
c. describe the various forms institutions take, and explain how they develop and change over time;
d. identify and analyze examples of tensions between expressions of individuality and efforts used to promote social conformity by groups and institutions;
e. describe and examine belief systems basic to specific traditions and laws in contemporary and historical movements;
f. evaluate the role of institutions in furthering both continuity and change;
g. analyze the extent to which groups and institutions meet individual needs and promote the common good in contemporary and historical settings;
h. explain and apply ideas and modes of inquiry drawn from behavioral science and social theory in the examination of persistent issues and social problems.

VI Power, Authority, and Governance

Social studies programs should include experiences that provide for the study of how people create and change structures of power, authority, and governance, so that the learner can:

a. examine persistent issues involving the rights, roles, and status of the individual in relation to the general welfare;
b. explain the purpose of government and analyze how its powers are acquired, used, and justified;
c. analyze and explain ideas and mechanisms to meet needs and wants of citizens, regulate territory, manage conflict, establish order and security, and balance competing conceptions of a just society;
d. compare and analyze the ways nations and organizations respond to conflicts between forces of unity and forces of diversity;
e. compare different political systems (their ideologies, structure, institutions, processes, and political cultures) with that of the United States, and identify representative political leaders from selected historical and contemporary settings;
f. analyze and evaluate conditions, actions, and motivations that contribute to conflict and cooperation within and among nations;
g. evaluate the role of technology in communications, transportation, information-processing, weapons development, or other areas as it contributes to or helps resolve conflicts;
h. explain and apply ideas, theories, and modes of inquiry drawn from political science to the examination of persistent issues and social problems;
i. evaluate the extent to which governments achieve their stated ideals and policies at home and abroad;
j. prepare a public policy paper and present and defend it before an appropriate forum in school or community.

VII Production, Distribution, and Consumption

Social studies programs should include experiences that provide for the study of how people organize for the production, distribution, and consumption of goods and services, so that the learner can:

a. explain how the scarcity of productive resources (human, capital, technological, and natural) requires the development of economic systems to make decisions about how goods and services are to be produced and distributed;
b. analyze the role that supply and demand, prices, incentives, and profits play in determining what is produced and distributed in a competitive market system;

APPENDIX

      c. consider the costs and benefits to society of allocating goods and services through private and public sectors;
      d. describe relationships among the various economic institutions that make up economic systems such as households, business firms, banks, government agencies, labor unions, and corporations;
      e. analyze the role of specialization and exchange in economic processes;
      f. compare how values and beliefs influence economic decisions in different societies;
      g. compare basic economic systems according to how rules and procedures deal with demand, supply, prices, the role of government, banks, labor and labor unions, savings and investments, and capital;
      h. apply economic concepts and reasoning when evaluating historical and contemporary social developments and issues;
      i. distinguish between the domestic and global economic systems, and explain how the two interact;
      j. apply knowledge of production, distribution, and consumption in the analysis of a public issue such as the allocation of health care or the consumption of energy, and devise an economic plan for accomplishing a socially desirable outcome related to that issue;
      k. distinguish between economics as a field of inquiry and the economy.

VIII   Science, Technology, and Society

Social studies programs should include experiences that provide for the study of relationships among science, technology, and society, so that the learner can:

      a. identify and describe both current and historical examples of the interaction and interdependence of science, technology, and society in a variety of cultural settings;
      b. make judgements about how science and technology have transformed the physical world and human society and our understanding of time, space, place, and human-environment interactions;
      c. analyze how science and technology influence the core values, beliefs, and attitudes of society, and how core values, beliefs, and attitudes of society shape scientific and technological change;
      d. evaluate various policies that have been proposed as ways of dealing with social changes resulting from new technologies, such as genetically engineered plants and animals;
      e. recognize and interpret varied perspectives about human societies and the physical world using scientific knowledge, ethical standards, and technologies from diverse world cultures;
      f. formulate strategies and develop policies for influencing public discussions associated with technology-society issues, such as the greenhouse effect.

IX   Global Connections

Social studies programs should include experiences that provide for the study of global connections and interdependence, so that the learner can:

      a. explain how language, art, music, belief systems, and other cultural elements can facilitate global understanding or misunderstanding;
      b. explain conditions and motivations that contribute to conflict, cooperation, and interdependence among groups, societies, and nations;
      c. analyze and evaluate the effects of changing technologies on the global community;
      d. analyze the causes, consequences, and possible solutions to persistent, contemporary, and emerging global issues, such as health, security, resource allocation, economic development, and environmental quality;
      e. analyze the relationships and tensions between national sovereignty and global interests, in such matters as territory, economic development, nuclear and other weapons, use of natural resources, and human rights concerns;
      f. analyze or formulate policy statements demonstrating an understanding of concerns, standards, issues, and conflicts related to universal human rights;
      g. describe and evaluate the role of international and multinational organizations in the global arena;
      h. illustrate how individual behaviors and decisions connect with global systems.

X Civic Ideals and Practices

Social studies programs should include experiences that provide for the study of the ideals, principles, and practices of citizenship in a democratic republic, so that the learner can:

 a. explain the origins and interpret the continuing influence of key ideals of the democratic republican form of government, such as individual human dignity, liberty, justice, equality, and the rule of law;
 b. identify, analyze, interpret, and evaluate sources and examples of citizens' rights and responsibilities;
 c. locate, access, analyze, organize, synthesize, evaluate, and apply information about selected public issues—identifying, describing, and evaluating multiple points of view;
 d. practice forms of civic discussion and participation consistent with the ideals of citizens in a democratic republic;
 e. analyze and evaluate the influence of various forms of citizen action on public policy;
 f. analyze a variety of public policies and issues from the perspective of formal and informal political actors;
 g. evaluate the effectiveness of public opinion in influencing and shaping public policy development and decision making;
 h. evaluate the degree to which public policies and citizen behaviors reflect or foster the stated ideals of a democratic republican form of government;
 i. construct a policy statement and an action plan to achieve one or more goals related to an issue of public concern;
 j. participate in activities to strengthen the "common good," based upon careful evaluation of possible options for citizen action.

Reprinted with permission from Expectations of Excellence—Curriculum Standards for Social Studies, *published by the National Council for the Social Studies. Copyright ©1994.*